THE HISTORY
OF THIRD PARTIES

THE U.S. GOVERNMENT
HOW IT WORKS

★ ★ ★

THE U.S. GOVERNMENT
HOW IT WORKS

THE HISTORY OF THIRD PARTIES

VICKI COX

CHELSEA HOUSE
PUBLISHERS
An imprint of Infobase Publishing

The History of Third Parties

Chelsea House
An imprint of Infobase Publishing
132 West 31st Street
New York NY 10001

Library of Congress Cataloging-in-Publication Data
Cox, Vicki.
 The history of third parties / Vicki Cox.
   p. cm. — (The U.S. government: how it works)
 Includes bibliographical references and index.
 ISBN-13: 978-0-7910-9421-1 (hardcover)
 ISBN-10: 0-7910-9421-9 (hardcover)
 1. Third parties (United States politics)—History—Juvenile literature.
 2. United States—Politics and government—Juvenile literature. I. Title.
 II. Series.

 JK2261.C834 2007
 324.273'8—dc22   2006100704

Text design by James Scotto-Lavino
Cover design by Ben Peterson

Printed in the United States of America
Bang NMSG 10 9 8 7 6 5 4 3 2 1

This book is printed on acid-free paper.

CONTENTS

1

THE TIP OF
THE ICEBERG

The smell of tear gas drifted across America, sending citizens to both sides of law and order. The events of 1963 had stunned the nation. Civil rights workers demonstrated in support of black people's rights to drink at the same water fountain as whites, to sit in the same restaurants, and to be hired by the same businesses. They were arrested and beaten. Birmingham, Alabama, one of the country's most segregated cities, shut down. In May, police had turned on marchers there. Police dogs with bared teeth were sent lunging at young blacks, and fire hose blasts knocked down demonstrators. On June 12, civil rights worker Medgar Evers was killed outside his home.

Birmingham, Alabama, was the setting for many civil rights demonstrations in the 1960s. Above, Reverend Wyatt Tee Walker (center, holding bullhorn) stands on the roof of a car while speaking with a crowd gathered to protest recent bombings on black-owned property in 1962.

Less than 10 days later, three volunteers who were working to register black voters in Mississippi were murdered. In September, an explosion killed four black girls as they put on their choir robes in the basement of Birmingham's Sixteenth Street Baptist Church.

As sirens blared, the injured screamed, and guns fired, one man emerged from the smoke and gas. George Wallace was a short man with slicked-back hair and a snarl on his bulldog face. As Alabama's governor, he had helped stir up hatred between blacks and whites. The Alabama state archives contain his January 1963 inaugural speech, part of which reads, ". . . segregation today, segregation tomorrow, segregation forever." Six months later, he personally stood in the door of the segregated University of Alabama to bar two black students from registering for classes, defying federal court-ordered integration. He claimed that he was fighting for a state's right (rather than the federal government's right) to govern its citizens.

Many people called him a demagogue. One told a *Time* magazine reporter who covered civil rights, "There wouldn't be any trouble if Wallace had stayed out. Why did he do it? Why didn't he leave us alone?" Other people admired how Wallace had defied the federal government. As the 1964 election approached, many urged Wallace to run for president.

Wallace told reporters that he had received nearly half a million letters. The *Time* article quoted letters that said, "Stand up, George, we are still behind you," "Thank God for your guts," and "You have my vote in the Presidential election."

Wallace realized that he had tapped into a great frustration and anger among Americans, and he entered presidential primaries in Wisconsin, Indiana, and Maryland as a Democrat to test Northern support. Surprisingly, he received 34 percent of the vote in Wisconsin, 42 percent in Maryland, and nearly that in Indiana. Still, he withdrew from the race, deciding to wait until 1968 to campaign again. A July 31, 1964, *Time* article took its title, "I was the Instrument," from what he said: "My mission has been accomplished. My purpose was to help conservatize both national parties. Today, we hear more talk of states' rights than we have heard in the past quarter century. I was the instrument through which the message was sent to the high council of the parties."

Wallace had a problem, though: the incumbent, President Lyndon Johnson, was automatically the Democratic nominee in 1968, and he controlled the Democrats' power and money. Wallace had no choice but to form a third party if he wanted to run.

Third parties always have difficulties. First, getting enough petition signatures to qualify for the ballot is a challenging task. Different rules and deadlines apply to each state. In North Dakota, Wallace supporters only needed 300 signatures to qualify. Yet, in Ohio, they needed more than 400,000. In California, 66,000 people actually had to leave their current parties and register as members of Wallace's party, the American Independent Party.

Second, many people believe that third party candidates stand no chance against the major parties. They assume that voting for a third party candidate simply throws their votes away.

Third, running a national campaign is expensive. Federal funding is available only to parties that received at least 5 percent of the popular vote in the previous election. Many who want to organize a third party simply do not have the millions of dollars necessary to run a modern campaign themselves.

These obstacles did not stop Wallace—and others—from forming a third party. The Communist Party and the Socialist Party formed because people have completely different views about how governments should run. The Progressives of 1912 and the Dixiecrats of 1948 broke away from established Republicans and Democrats because they disagreed with the major parties' decisions. Some third parties, such as Wallace's American Independent Party, organized around an individual. Other third parties organize around a single issue; it might be as silly as crusading for immediate contact with aliens from outer space or as personal as making everyone vegetarians. More often, third parties are concerned about who has the ultimate authority: the federal government or the 50 individual states. Wallace campaigned loudly and belligerently for states' rights.

When he spoke at a university or civic organization, his appearance was a combination of old-time revival, country-western show, and political advertisement. A band played country music and "God Bless America," and entertainers sang popular song tunes with lyrics written to praise Wallace. As an aide introduced him, volunteers passed buckets through the crowd for donations. When writing "Wallace's Army" for an October 18, 1986, *Time* magazine article, a reporter watched Wallace shake hands with admirers after his speech. They said, "You're the only hope for America." He replied, "Thank y'all for heppin' us." Wallace did not talk about segregation (or race) as he campaigned, but he attacked the Civil Rights

George Wallace speaks from the steps of the Capitol in Albany, New York, during a campaign stop in 1968. Although Wallace did not stand a chance of winning the presidential election, he is credited with affecting the issues discussed that year.

Act, then under debate in Congress. His message centered on how the federal government had stomped on states' rights and intruded into the private lives of individuals.

In his biography of Wallace, Stephan Lesher described how both supporters and critics showed up to his appearances, making any Wallace appearance a tinderbox waiting to ignite. Anywhere from 3,000 to 25,000 supporters would show up to cheer him. They liked to hear him talk about the "pseudo-intellectuals" and college professors who drew tax-dollar salaries while opposing the Vietnam War. Lesher included Wallace's speeches about the nation's lawlessness that stated, "You can't even walk in the shadow of the White House in Washington, D.C., unless you got two police dogs with you." He declared that he would make the streets safe again even if he "had to keep thirty thousand troops standing on the streets two feet apart and with two-foot-long bayonets."

According to Lesher's book, at a police officers' national convention he claimed that if police "were allowed to carry out the law and were backed up by the judges and the courts they would cut out the tremendous increase in crime on the streets." Criticizing the court system, he said, "When you get hit over the head, the man who hit you will be free before you even get to the hospital."

A *Newsweek* article titled "The Spoiler" noted that Wallace "talks about the two parties as tweedledum and tweedledee, raises hell with the Supreme Court and pseudo-intellectuals (and professors) with pointed heads who can't even park their bicycles straight."

Many supporters thought that Wallace spoke for them. Lesher reported that one voter said, "You don't have to worry about figuring out where he stands. He tells it like it really is." Others said, "Wallace is the man to straighten this country out," and "He's the only one who is really for law and order."

Lesher included many details about those who opposed Wallace. Critics jeered, booed, hissed, stamped their feet, chanted, and heckled him. He was pelted with pennies, popsicles, tomatoes, and rocks. At Dartmouth College, a mob of 500 students pinned him in his car after a rally, rocking and banging it. Lesher told that, at another rally, protesters headed toward the stage with signs that read "Racist, Go Home" and "Wallace Doesn't Have Anything against Negroes—He Thinks Everybody Should Own One." Someone yelled, "They're coming to lynch you, Wallace!" Wallace's enemies attacked his segregationist views, calling him a "clown," "a kook," and "a buffoon." Others called him a "bigot."

Wallace didn't mind the name calling. According to a *Newsweek* article (titled "The Rattle of Eyeteeth"), "I thought I would be ignored, but instead I am getting more publicity than a man could buy."

The disturbances gave Wallace a chance to criticize his critics. When hecklers threw objects at him, the *Newsweek* reporter wrote, Wallace retorted, "There are the folks that people like us are sick and tired of. You've been getting a good lesson in what we've been talking about. They talk about free speech but won't allow it to others." Another article ("Wallace's Army: The Coalition of Frustration") appeared in the October 18, 1968, issue of *Time*. It reported that Wallace would say to hecklers, "When I get through speaking, you can come up here and I'll autograph your sandals."

The American Independent Party grew. In Texas, where Wallace needed only 14,000 signatures to get on the ballot, he got 98,000. In Georgia, where he needed 84,000, he got 180,000. Eventually, he qualified for the ballot in all 50 states.

Lesher's biography included Wallace's opinion of his popularity. He said, "I'm more attuned to the people. I know a lot more about what and how they're thinking than anybody else who wants to be president. I know they're tired of what has been going on."

Wallace knew that people, including taxi cab drivers, hairdressers, and factory workers all over the country, felt helpless. They felt that no leader cared about them and they were afraid of antiwar demonstrators and civil rights protests. After Martin Luther King Jr. and President John F. Kennedy were assassinated, they feared for their own lives.

Lesher showed that Wallace sympathized. "I'm sick and tired of some professors and some preachers and some judges and some newspaper editors having more to say about my every day life . . . than I have to say about it myself," he said.

He opposed civil rights, voting rights, open housing, and busing for integration. Never mentioning race, he preached that federal laws had taken control of the ordinary man's life. His supporters were people who worked hard and were afraid of losing what they had: union members who feared that they would lose their seniority because of quota hiring; homeowners who feared that their property value would decrease as blacks moved into white neighborhoods; mothers who did not want their children bused across town to integrate schools. According to Lesher, Wallace said, "A vote for this little governor will let people in Washington know that we want them to leave our house, schools, jobs, businesses, and farms alone—and let us run them without any help from Washington."

The media created the Wallace phenomenon. Usually, third parties don't get much publicity. In this case, though, the media reported almost everything that Wallace said and did. He was on national talk shows and on the covers of national magazines. The fights between his admirers and enemies, his colorful language, and his one-line put-downs of hecklers made great stories.

Wallace took full advantage of the publicity. He arrived in a town in the morning, shook hands with every spectator who greeted him, and held a press conference so that his quotes would be used in the afternoon or evening news. He went to the local radio and television stations and talked to anyone who would listen. In the evening, he spoke at rallies. Twenty-five years later, other candidates for office would use his techniques.

In reality, no third-party candidate has ever had a chance of winning the presidency, and the American Independent Party was no different. A third party candidate can greatly affect the outcome of an election, however. Simply by getting enough electoral delegates, Wallace could prevent either major party from winning the election. Then he could negotiate with candidates, exchanging his electoral delegates for things he wanted. He could pledge his delegates to the one who would let states run their schools as they wished—even if it meant that schools were segregated. He might insist that hospitals be free to decide who used which bathrooms. He might even demand that homeowners be allowed to sell their houses only to people (or the race of people) they liked.

An October 18, 1968, *Time* article reported that, as the election neared, Wallace's Republican opponent, Richard M. Nixon, did two things that major parties often do to third parties. First, he played the wasted-vote strategy. Nixon asked a Michigan crowd, "Do you want to make a point, or do you want to make a change?" Then, noticing how voters liked Wallace's law and order theme, Nixon adopted it into his own campaign.

In the November 1968 elections, Wallace carried five states—Alabama, Georgia, Louisiana, Mississippi, and Arkansas—for 45 electoral votes. Those who analyze electoral numbers believed that Wallace had been a spoiler, taking votes from Democrat Hubert Humphrey and allowing Nixon to win.

Newsweek's May 18, 1967, article reported Wallace's post-election remarks. He did not sound as if he had lost: "The movement has already won," he said. "Both national parties have changed direction because of our movement."

Political analysts were not so sure that Wallace and the American Independent Party were washed up, either. Lesher wrote that someone had said, "Wallace is a campaigner, and a good one. He is a politician, and a first-rate one. Above all else, he is an authentic spokesman for millions of Americans."

He was not the only American who wanted the central government limited and who thought that Communists and students were attacking democracy. According to Lesher, Wallace said, "My vote was only the tip of an iceberg."

Without Wallace's taking office himself, many of the issues that he cared about became part of the major parties' philosophies. Wallace's American Independent Party accomplished what other third parties have done throughout the country's history: Without winning, they forced the major parties to examine more closely what voters wanted.

2

A Dirty, Nasty Business

Politics is often said to be a dirty business. Since the founding of the United States, arguments over government have made enemies of good friends and unreasonable bigots out of intelligent men. The hostilities began the moment America was formed.

Despite their wigs, silk stockings, and dignified appearance in oil paintings, the Founding Fathers were rebels. They believed so strongly in their vision of good government that they started a war for their beliefs. After independence was won, those intense feelings centered on balancing the authority of individual states with the authority of the federal government.

The Founding Fathers did not like the idea of political parties (or factions, as they were called). In his book

Like the other Founding Fathers, Thomas Jefferson *(above)* was opposed to political parties. Regardless, when he ran for president, he campaigned as a member of the Republican Party.

The Democrats From Jefferson to Carter, Robert Rutland reported that both John Adams and Thomas Jefferson had strong opinions about political parties. In 1789, according to Rutland's book, John Adams said that dividing

Americans into parties was to be feared as "the greatest political evil under our Constitution." Thomas Jefferson put it more strongly, "If I could not go to Heaven but with a party, I would not go there at all."

At first, when disagreements arose, there were no political parties to criticize. Arguments and name-calling occurred between individuals. In Carl Byker's PBS program "The Duel," historian Joanne Freeman explained, "without parties, without team rules of fighting, politics ended up being very personal, based on character and reputation. The personal and political mixed in with each other in an ultimately dangerous kind of way."

Plotting and scheming began early on. Although everyone agreed that George Washington should be president, an election was held anyway. Alexander Hamilton, who greatly admired Washington, secretly met with electors to ask them to withhold one of their two votes, some of which were to go to Washington's opponent John Adams, in order to enlarge Washington's margin of victory. As a result, Adams received only 34 votes to Washington's 69. In his book *John Adams*, author David McCullough wrote that, when Adams learned of Hamilton's crusade, he called it a "dark and dirty intrigue," complaining, "Is not my election to this office in the scurvy manner in which it was done a curse rather than a blessing?"

FEDERALISTS AND REPUBLICANS

It did not take long for America's leaders to separate into two groups. Each believed it would preserve the country, and its opponents would destroy it. Alexander

Although Alexander Hamilton *(above)* was never elected president, he was one of the most influential Founding Fathers. Hamilton led the Federalist Party, one of the first political parties in the new United States.

Hamilton led the Federalists, and Thomas Jefferson headed the Republicans. These were not hard-core political parties—yet. Representatives who voted in Congress rarely followed an official party line, and the arguing remained extremely personal.

Except for the election of George Washington, the Founding Fathers disagreed about everything—even what to call their new president. Federalists proposed "His Highness, the President of the United States of America, and Protector of the rights of the Same." Rutland wrote that Thomas Jefferson called the suggested title "the most superlatively ridiculous thing I ever heard of."

The heart of most arguments concerned the role of the federal government in what could just barely be called a nation. The army consisted of about 700 men, roads were terrible, and wages were low. Individual states printed their own money, and British, French, and Spanish coins mixed in with it, varying in value from state to state. The entire country had only three banks. States felt little loyalty to the union. McCullough's book quoted a letter from General Nathanael Greene to Washington that stated, "Many people secretly wish that every state be completely independent and that as soon as our public debts are liquidated that Congress should be no more."

Alexander Hamilton had other ideas. He favored a strong federal government that was run by educated and wealthy men. He proposed that it pay the individual states' war debts, believing that the more responsibility it assumed, the more authority it would have. He wanted a national bank that was funded by tariffs and loans made by the wealthy, giving them a stake in the nation's survival. Hamilton also wanted a large army and navy for national security, and he and his Federalist friends favored a constitution similar to England's.

Thomas Jefferson and James Madison feared that Hamilton's government would become just as tyrannical as England's had been. With Hamilton favoring commerce and industry over farming (mostly in the South), they also feared that the Southern states would get fed up and secede from the union. Republicans wanted strong state governments that took care of their citizens and a federal government that stayed out of the affairs of individuals and the states. In *Alexander Hamilton, American*, Richard Brookhiser wrote that Jefferson believed in the common man, proclaiming that "those who labor in the earth are the chosen people of God." He and his friends opposed a large military, fearing that it might eventually try to overthrow the government.

Hamilton, as secretary of the treasury, and Jefferson, as secretary of state, became bitter enemies. Their followers soon used newspapers to publicize their ideas. Hamilton wrote many articles that explained Federalist philosophy in *The Gazette of the United States*.

In 1791, Jefferson hired Philip Freneau as translator in the State Department in Philadelphia. In his "spare" time, Freneau organized the *National Gazette*, which sometimes criticized Washington (an almost treasonous action), "just happened" to frequently attack Hamilton's Federalists, and "just happened" to praise Jefferson's Republicans.

Hamilton exposed the connection, implying that Jefferson did not like Washington, and he hinted that the

ELECTING THE PRESIDENT

Early in U.S. history, the system for electing the president and vice president was different from the one we use today. Electors, who were chosen by each state's legislature, voted from a list of presidential hopefuls. Each electoral member voted for two candidates. One vote, everyone supposed, would go to a personal favorite or a person from the elector's state. The other would go to the most qualified and realistic candidate. Whoever got the majority of votes became president; the runner-up became vice president. In the event of a tie among electors, according to this early plan, the House of Representatives named the president.

The 1796 election proved why the procedure was flawed. By this time, the country had divided into two intensely conflicting factions: the Federalists and the Republicans. The 1796 election ended with John Adams, a Federalist, being elected president and Thomas Jefferson, who held republican ideas about government, being elected vice president. With their strongly felt opposing ideas about government, they did not, or could not, work together.

In 1800, Jefferson and Aaron Burr, both of the same party, tied for the presidency. It took five days and 36 votes before Jefferson finally became the nation's third president. He won by one vote. Congress quickly passed the Twelfth Amendment to the Constitution, giving electors only one vote for president and a completely separate vote for vice president. The Electoral College is still governed by the Twelfth Amendment today, though it is now assumed that candidates for president and vice president who run on the same ticket will be elected together.

association between Freneau and Jefferson was improper. He conveniently forgot the government documents that he "just happened" to order from the *National Gazette*.

Washington asked the men to stop quarreling, but they did not. Hamilton continued to print attacks on Jefferson under pseudonyms. In *John Adams*, David McCullough wrote that Jefferson was called a "closet politician"; he worked behind the scenes to oust Hamilton from office and wrote to Madison, "For God's sake, my dear sir, take up your pen, select the most striking heresies, and cut him to pieces in the face of the public."

With Washington's retirement, the 1796 election was a free-for-all. Jefferson was the Republican presidential candidate. The Federalists had their own agenda. According to Noble Cunningham in *The Jeffersonian Republicans: The Formation of Party Organization 1789–1801,* Hamilton wrote, "Everything must give way to the great object of excluding Jefferson."

The Republican papers attacked Vice President Adams as the Federalist frontrunner. McCullough's *John Adams* included their cruel descriptions: The papers labeled him "the champion of kings, ranks, and titles." They ridiculed his weight, calling him "His Rotundity" and criticized his "sesquipedality of belly." In turn, Federalist newspapers warned that Jefferson was an atheist and a coward for running from the British in 1781.

Noble Cunningham's book was not the only one to record Jefferson's observations on party loyalties. Jefferson noticed Philadelphians "who had been intimate all their lives, cross the streets to avoid meeting, and turn their heads another way, lest they should be obliged to touch their hats."

John Adams defeated Jefferson by three electoral votes, so Jefferson became vice president. Having a Federalist president and a Republican vice president was like having the three little pigs and big, bad wolf live in the same house. Jefferson, who had been a minister to France, might have proven valuable to Adams in a complex quasi-war with France. McCullough observed, however, that Adams never asked for Jefferson's advice, nor, as Jefferson wrote, "ever consulted me as to any measures of the government."

The Republicans kept busy discrediting Federalists. James Callender, a tabloid-type writer for the Republican *Aurora*, broke the story of Hamilton's affair with Maria Reynolds in 1797 and also accused Hamilton of embezzling government funds. Hamilton proved that he had done nothing improper as treasury secretary, but he was center of the country's first sex scandal. In opposing the president's handling of the war with the French, however, the Republicans saved their most vicious comments for Adams. McCullough said that they questioned his sanity, calling him a man "divested of his senses."

In 1798, Adams and the Federalists passed the Alien and Sedition Acts. Although supposedly written to protect the country from French and Irish spies, they were really aimed at Republicans. This law made it illegal to publicly criticize the president or other government officials until March 3, 1801—after the next election. Several newspapermen were jailed, and a Vermont congressman was fined $1,000.

Citizens were outraged; some considered taking up arms to overturn the law. Even the vice president schemed against the president. In *John Adams*, McCullough wrote that, working behind the scenes, Jefferson drafted the Kentucky Resolutions, which declared that the states could overturn any unconstitutional law passed by Congress. He felt so strongly about the rights of states that he told Madison he was "determined . . . to sever ourselves from the Union we so much value, rather than give up the rights of self-government."

The election of 1800 was one of the most vicious in American history. The two parties were, by then, permanently entrenched in the country, and thus the Federalist president ran against the Republican vice president.

In *John Adams*, McCullough described how the parties smeared each other: Federalists called Jefferson a "weakling" and a "spendthrift" and warned that Christians would need to hide their family Bibles if the "godless" Jefferson were elected. Republicans described Adams as "a repulsive pedant," "a gross hypocrite," and "one of the most egregious fools upon the continent." They accused him of sending for British mistresses for himself and another official. Hamilton, who should have supported a fellow Federalist, blasted Adams's "intrinsic defects of

THE DUEL: A QUESTION OF CHARACTER

The most famous duel in American history resulted in the death of Alexander Hamilton, one of the country's most brilliant men, and in the disgrace of the country's vice president, Aaron Burr. The two men had been bitter enemies for 15 years. Hamilton hated Burr because he defeated Hamilton's father-in law for a Senate seat in New York and because Burr seemed to care more for his own ambitions than for the welfare of the country. Burr hated Hamilton because he campaigned against Burr, a fellow Federalist, when Jefferson and Burr tied in the 1800 election. Hamilton's influence caused the presidency to go to Jefferson. To hang onto his political career, Burr ran for governor of New York. Hamilton rode on horseback across the state to tell Federalists that they should vote for the devil himself rather than for Burr. Burr lost. Humiliated, he attempted to restore his honor by challenging Hamilton to a duel on a field of honor. Hamilton, according to some, fired first and purposely missed Burr. Burr was not so kind. He shot Hamilton in the stomach, and Hamilton died 36 hours later. Instead of reestablishing his reputation with the duel, Burr killed his own career. Outrage at Hamilton's death crisscrossed the country, and Burr never again was powerful in politics.

character," "his disgusting egotism," and his "ungovernable temper." The Federalists' infighting split their vote, and Adams finished a distant third.

In the end, Jefferson tied with Aaron Burr. According to the Constitution, the election was decided in the House of Representatives. Hamilton, who hated Burr more than he hated Jefferson, threw his influence to Jefferson. McCullough reported in *John Adams* that Jefferson, who had ridiculed Adams as "the President by three votes," himself won by only a single vote.

As president, Jefferson replaced many Federalist ideas with Republican ones. He repealed the Alien and Sedition Acts, freed its prisoners and returned its fines, downsized the army, slashed the national budget in half, and eliminated domestic taxes. Ironically, this "president of the common man," who answered the door of the White House in house slippers, owned hundreds of slaves and drank the finest French wines.

TERTIUM QUIDS

By 1806, Jefferson's activities so upset members of his Republican Party that a group split away from it. The nation's first third party, the Tertium Quids, believed that Jefferson had betrayed the supremacy of states and had become a dreadful Federalist, and that he overstepped the president's role by authorizing the Louisiana Purchase.

The Tertium Quids was led by Virginian John Randolph. About their rivals, Randolph wrote a letter to an ally stating: "The Administration . . . favors federal principles, and, with the exception of a few great rival characters, federal men. . . . The old republican party is already ruined, past redemption."

More like a gnat buzzing around giants, the Tertium Quids exerted little influence on the two major parties. They tried to prevent the election of James Madison by supporting James Monroe in 1808, but they failed.

3

ABOLITION

As much as slavery, land was the wind that ignited the Civil War. Both North and South needed the West, but for very different reasons.

The South had overfarmed its land: In *Free Soil, Free Labor, Free Men*, Eric Foner wrote that, while traveling through the region, William E. Seward saw "an exhausted soil, old and decaying towns, wretchedly-neglected roads, an absence of enterprise and improvement. . . . If the South controlled the new western territories, it would fill up the area with large plantations and slaves to work them."

The North, too, thought that the new territories would solve its problems. First, the North was drowning in immigrants. With too many laborers for available jobs, its wages were very low. The North wanted workers to move west to make room for those who arrived daily from Europe. Second, the North did not think that

Southern lifestyles fit America's new image as an industrious, energetic country. Held against their will, slaves had no reason to work hard, and Northerners believed in hard work. Northern laborers might take menial jobs, but they eventually bettered themselves, started new businesses, and became more educated. Northerners believed that educated men would improve the country, making America a world leader. Thus, the North and the South both cast eager eyes on the West and the country's future.

The North supported the 1787 Northwest Ordinance, which barred slavery from new territories. The South opposed it. With 11 states in the Senate for each region, Congress wanted to maintain the balance. In 1820, the Missouri Compromise allowed the territory of Maine to enter as a "free" state and Missouri to enter as a "slave" state. Except for Missouri, the Compromise also barred slaves north of the latitude line of 36 degrees, 30 minutes.

THE LIBERTY PARTY

By this time, the Federalists and Republicans had merged, split apart, and reappeared with several different names. National Republicans (with Hamilton's view of a strong federal government) became Whigs. Democratic-Republicans (with Jefferson's republican view of strong states' rights) became Democrats. Regardless of their names, the parties could not agree among themselves on slavery.

In 1840, New York abolitionists, many of them ministers, formed the Liberty Party specifically to oppose slavery. They believed that slavery was a sin against both God and man. They quoted scripture to denounce slavery and printed verses on Liberty Party voting tickets. Making slavery a moral issue did not really work: Their presidential candidate, James G. Birney, got only 7,000 votes in the 1840 election.

Salmon P. Chase convinced the Liberty Party to expand its arguments beyond religion. According to Foner's book *Free Soil, Free Labor, Free Men,* Chase said, "Freedom is national; slavery only is local and sectional."

The Liberty Party presented slavery as an issue of states' rights versus the federal government. It argued that a state could make slavery lawful, but under the Constitution, slavery could not be recognized anywhere under federal control. Because the federal government controlled the new territories, the Liberty Party wanted slavery banned there. It also proposed that slaves who escaped to an area controlled by the federal government were free.

The Liberty Party did better in 1844, receiving 62,000 votes. While a third party candidate did not win, the party did influence the election. Birney, again the Liberty Party's candidate, took enough votes from Henry Clay in New York to throw the election to James K. Polk.

FREE SOIL PARTY

Four years later, in Buffalo, New York, the Liberty Party merged with other antislavery factions to form the Free Soil Party. One of the groups that merged was the Conscience Whigs, a group that split off from the Whigs.

Martin Van Buren *(above),* who had served one term as president (1833–1837), ran again in 1848. That time, however, he ran as a third-party candidate from the Free Soil Party. He was unsuccessful in his presidential bid.

Antislavery Democrats who also joined were called "Barnburners." Their nickname came from a Dutch farmer who burned down his barn to rid it of rats. The Free Soil Party rallied around the slogan "Free Soil, Free Speech, Free Labor, and Free Men." In the *Encyclopedia of Third Parties in the United States,* Earl Kruschke stated that its purpose was to "maintain the rights of Free Labor against the aggressions of the Slave Power and to secure Free Soil for a Free People."

Like the Liberty Party, the Free Soil Party believed that the Constitution said that the federal government could not deny freedom to anyone. Its platform, Kruschke wrote, said that "Congress has no more power to make a slave than to make a king; no more power to institute or establish slavery, than to institute or establish a monarchy."

The Free Soil Party's planks included free homesteads and no more slave states or territories. They supported a tariff, river and harbor improvements, and lower postage rates. The Free Soil Party's nominee, Martin Van Buren, received nearly 300,000 popular votes. Although he did not win any electoral votes, his numbers gave the presidency to Zachary Taylor rather than to Democratic nominee Lewis Cass. Voters elected Salmon P. Chase, the leader of the Free Soilers, to the U.S. Senate, and nine other Free Soilers to the House of Representatives.

The Compromise of 1850 inflamed regional tensions further. California, rich with gold, entered the Union as a free state. To make up for tipping the balance toward free states, Congress passed the Fugitive Slave Act. This act

In the first part of the nineteenth century, much of the political debate focused on the issue of slavery, which was allowed in some states and not in others. In the illustration above, fugitive slaves travel the Underground Railroad in search of freedom.

denied escaped slaves the right to jury trials, giving special commissioners authority over them. The commissioners were paid 5 dollars if the fugitive was released and 10 dollars if the owner got the slave back. It was not hard to guess how they usually ruled. Federal officials enforced the law, so citizens had to return runaway slaves. Abolitionists were enraged.

In 1851, the Free Soil Party reorganized as the Free Democratic Party and officially denounced the Compromise of 1850. It demanded "no more slave States, no slave territory, no nationalized slavery, and no national legislation for the extradition of slaves," said Kruschke's *Encyclopedia of Third Parties in the United States.*

Kruschke also said that the Free Soil Party wanted western lands to go to the people, not to big corporations. The party claimed that "all men have a natural right to a portion of the soil; and that, as the use of the soil is indispensable to life, the right of all men to the soil is as sacred as their right to life itself." Its candidate received only 155,210 popular votes. Franklin Pierce (a Democrat) was elected, the Whig Party disappeared, and the Free Soil Party joined the newly organized Republicans.

Two events harmed the antislavery cause. In 1854, the Kansas-Nebraska Act repealed the 1820 Missouri Compromise, prohibiting slavery north of 36 degrees, 30 minutes latitude. The Kansas-Nebraska Act allowed territories to decide the slave issue themselves by popular sovereignty. The North was dismayed. The South happily thought that slavery would spread into the West. The second event that upset abolitionists was the *Dred Scott* case. Before 1857, the Constitution had not protected slavery. Dred Scott, a slave, and his master, an army officer, moved from the slave state of Missouri to the free state of Illinois and then to Northern free territory. Later, they returned to Missouri. Scott claimed that he was free because he had lived on free soil.

The Supreme Court disagreed: In March 1845, it declared that no slave or a slave's descendant had ever been—or could ever be—a U.S. citizen. As "beings of an inferior order," they were not included in the Declaration of Independence statement that "all men are created equal." Scott was a slave who would never have rights. The decision deepened the battle lines between North and South.

AMERICAN PARTY (THE KNOW-NOTHINGS)

As if the slavery issue were not enough to incite the country, nativists tapped into ethnic prejudices. The Order of the Star Spangled Banner and the Order of United Americans hated immigrants. These groups thought that immigrants were morally bankrupt lowlifes who caused poverty and political corruption. They feared that, through priests, the pope would tell the many Irish immigrants how to vote and believed that all immigrants took jobs from native-born workers. Fearing that "foreigners" were polluting a "pure" America, the American Party formed in the 1840s.

When outsiders asked about the party, members answered, "I know nothing," and the group became known as the Know-Nothings. Members were native-born Protestants whose spouses were not Catholic. They wanted immigrants to wait 21 years before becoming U.S. citizens and did not want foreigners or Catholics to hold public office. "Save the Union" was their rallying cry. Along with nativist literature, they promoted "Know-Nothing Candy," "Know-Nothing Tea," and "Know-Nothing Toothpicks."

The American Party (or Know-Nothings) attracted people who were upset by the Whig party and by the Democratic association with Irish Americans. Membership swelled from 50,000 to more than a million.

JOHN BROWN

* * * * *

Some think that John Brown was a dedicated crusader against slavery. Others believe that he was a terrorist. Brown is best known for his attack at Harpers Ferry, Virginia, when he and 21 men seized a federal arsenal, planning to distribute weapons stored there to slaves.

Brown had long been an abolitionist. He gave land to fugitive slaves and participated in the Underground Railroad. A year after the Fugitive Slave Act was passed, he helped found the League of Gileadites, an organization that protected escaped slaves from bounty hunters.

Frederick Douglass, an abolitionist and former slave, regarded Brown "as deeply interested in our cause, as though his own soul had been pierced with the iron of slavery."* Brown told Douglass his plan to start a war to free the slaves. Five of Brown's sons also moved to Kansas territory. The Kansas-Nebraska Act allowed settlers to decide the slavery issue themselves, and both sides jammed the area with sympathetic settlers.

After Kansas appeared to be heading toward becoming a free state, proslavery forces became violent. Brown's sons wrote to their father, asking for guns to protect themselves. In October 1855, Brown brought them weapons himself. Fearful that his sons were marked for attack by the proslavery supporters, Brown struck on May 24, 1856, capturing five proslavery men and hacking them to death with broadswords in what became known as the Pottawatomie Massacre. Six months later, Brown inflicted heavy casualties on 300 Missouri Bushwhackers who were intent on destroying free-state settlements in Kansas. Both of these incidents brought Brown national attention.

Brown raided Harpers Ferry, intending to use the 100,000 muskets and rifles stored there for a war against slavery in the South. On October 16, 1859, Brown's forces took the armory from the single watchman, cut the telegraph lines, and captured hostages on nearby farms. They allowed an eastbound train to pass through the town, however, which spread word of the attack.

Within 36 hours, Brown was captured by U.S. Marines led by Lieutenant Colonel Robert E. Lee. Brown was tried for murder, treason against Virginia, and inspiring a slave rebellion. He was convicted and sentenced to be hanged. During the month he awaited execution, Brown wrote many letters to explain his willingness to die for the abolitionist cause. Northern newspapers printed them, and the South was infuriated. The North began to view the abolitionist Brown more favorably. "No man in America has ever stood up so persistently and effectively for the dignity of human nature," said Henry David Thoreau.**

Brown was hanged on December 2, 1859. Among those guarding him at his execution was John Wilkes Booth, who would later assassinate President Lincoln. Brown's hanging dramatized the hopelessness of a peaceful settlement between North and South. The Civil War began 16 months later.

---

*"Mass Moments: John Brown Speaks in Concord." http://www.massmoments .org/moment.cfm?mid=78.

**"John Brown's Holy War." The American Experience. PBS. http://www.pbs.org/ wgbh/amex/brown/peopleevents/pande01.html.

The Know-Nothings enjoyed some success. They controlled the New York and Massachusetts legislatures and elected several governors and mayors and about 90 congressmen, more than any third party. One member, Nathaniel Banks, was the only third-party Speaker of the House.

Simply being anti-Catholic and anti-immigration could not hold the party together, however. After the Kansas-Nebraska Act was passed, antislavery members abandoned the Know-Nothings and became Republicans. Proslavery Know-Nothings pushed through a proslavery resolution and nominated Millard Fillmore for president in 1856. Its platform, according to Kruschke's *Encyclopedia of Third Parties in the United States*, stated that "Americans must rule America; and to this end, native-born citizens should be selected for all state, federal, or municipal offices of government employment, in preference to naturalized citizens. . . . " Fillmore won only Maryland.

THE CONSTITUTIONAL UNION PARTY

In 1859, border-state dissidents formed the Constitutional Union Party. With the bitterness between the North and the South, its members were called "bellringers" because their one goal was to preserve the Union and return to the ways of the past. Its presidential candidate, Tennessee's John Bell, received 590,901 votes and Kentucky's 39 electoral votes. When war broke out, this one-issue third party dissolved.

In 1860, the course of American history changed because of a splinter third party. The Democrats nominated
Stephen A. Douglas for president. They straddled the
slavery issue by supporting slavery in the South and
suggesting that the territories decide their position on it.
At the party convention in Charleston, South Carolina,
Southern Democrats objected, wanting the party to protect slavery in the territories. About 200 walked out and
then nominated their own presidential candidate, John
C. Breckinridge. Democratic voters thus chose between
Douglas and Breckinridge, two candidates with two plat-
forms and two different views concerning slavery in the
territories. The two groups split the Democratic vote, and
the Republican candidate won the presidency. That man
was Abraham Lincoln.

4

FIGHTING FOR
THE LITTLE GUY

Extraordinary changes took place between 1870 and 1912: America shifted from farms to cities, from agriculture to industry. The little guy—the ordinary farmer and laborer—was squashed by oil, steel, and railroad monopolies. Farmers were desperate because they had large debts. Fertile land produced too much corn and wheat, depressing the American market; new settlers kept planting; and European markets disappeared.

The PBS American Series program "1900" recounted what one dispirited farmer said: "We went to work and plowed and planted. The rains fell; the sun shone; nature smiled. And what came of it? 8 cent corn, 10 cent oats, 2 cent beef and no price at all for butter and eggs."

Railroads fixed prices on grain storage and transportation rates. They cheated while weighing crops and charged favored customers differently from ordinary customers.

THE GRANGE

In 1867, the National Grange of the Order of Patrons of Husbandry (or simply the Grange) formed. It organized cooperatives (co-ops) to fight railroad and eastern bank control. Members bought equipment together, deposited savings in farmer credit unions rather than in banks, and built grain elevators. Grangers, elected to state legislatures, passed Granger laws that regulated elevator and railroad rates. The railroads sued, and the Supreme Court later declared the laws unconstitutional. The Grange eventually faded, but it proved that organized farmers could follow a political agenda.

The Panic of 1873 slammed farmers who were already reeling under staggering debts. "Hard money," currency backed by a limited gold supply, was scarce. Farmers wanted the government to print greenbacks, like the $450 million it had printed during the Civil War. With no gold to back it, paper money was no more valuable than Monopoly money, but it was in limitless supply. Farmers believed that inflation would result, allowing them to borrow money in the spring for seed, sell produce at higher prices in the fall, and repay their debts with what an Internet article (at www.u-s-history.com) on the Greenback Party called " 'cheap' money."

DIRECT ELECTION OF SENATORS

The Framers who wrote the U.S. Constitution never intended for the people to elect their U.S. senators. Instead, they instructed the state legislatures to elect them, believing that state officials would be more loyal to federal officials if they chose them. The Framers also felt that the people would not be able to pressure their senators to vote for their special interests if they had no part in the senators' election.

Requests for election reform began to appear as early as 1826. Nearly every year from 1893 to 1902, a constitutional amendment was sent to Congress for direct election of senators. Senators vigorously rejected the idea. The result was that senate seats were often left empty because of infighting in state politics.

In 1892, the Populist Party wrote direct election of senators into its platform. The major parties ignored the issue. Gradually, the states themselves initiated reforms, and as more of the direct-election senators were sent to Congress, the issue gained enough support to pass a constitutional amendment.

The Seventeenth Amendment, passed in 1913, replaced the phrase "chosen by the Legislature thereof" with the phrase "elected by the people thereof." It also authorized the governor to fill a vacant senate seat until a general election could be called.

Wealthy creditors and eastern bankers, mostly Republicans, wanted payment in money backed by gold. In 1875, Congress passed the Specie Resumption Act,

The Panic of 1873 was a severe nationwide economic depression that lasted until 1877. The illustration above shows a common scene at the time: customers who rushed to their bank, desperate to claim their money before the bank shut down.

which matched the number of greenbacks to gold reserves. According to an Internet article (u-s-history .com) on the Specie Resumption Act of 1875, this made paper money "good as gold"—which did not help farmers.

THE GREENBACK PARTY

The Greenback Party pledged to fight the Specie Resumption Act. Peter Cooper ran as its presidential nominee in 1876. As a one-issue party, it received only 80,000 votes. Two years later, having added labor workers to its membership, the renamed Greenback-Labor Party received a million votes and elected 14 congressmen. In 1880, it widened its platform, calling for a graduated income tax, an eight-hour work day, elimination of child labor, exclusion of Chinese immigrants, and giving women the vote. The party's candidate received only 300,000 votes. It was obvious that printing unlimited money no longer interested voters. The party merged with the Populists in 1892.

THE POPULIST PARTY

In February 1892, farmers, unionists, and radicals formed a new third party, the Populist Party. An Internet article from the Douglass Archives (douglassarchives.org) quoted Ignatius Donnelly's statement of the party's purpose: "We seek to restore the government of the republic to the hands of the plain people with whom it originated."

The Populist Party platform crusaded for the little guy. It wanted the president, vice president, and senators to be elected directly by the people and railroad, telegraph, and telephone companies to be under government

William Jennings Bryan, called the "Boy Orator" because of
his youth and talent for public speaking, appeared during a
campaign event in 1896. He ran for president as a member
of the Democratic Party, but he did not win.

control. It supported child labor laws and an eight-hour
work day and called for lifting injunctions against unions.
The party also wanted a graduated income tax. To help
farmers, it suggested that money be based on both silver
and gold. Silver, worth 1 dollar per troy ounce to gold's
20 dollars, could put more money in circulation, and new
strikes in the West provided plenty. Inflation would drive
prices up, and produce could sell for more at the end of
the season.

Free coinage of silver originated with the Populists, but, like many third-party ideas, a major party noticed its popularity and stole it. On July 9, 1896, 36-year-old William Jennings Bryan, a little-known politician, addressed the Democratic convention. A talented speaker, he embraced the working man and free coinage of silver. His last words that day were his most famous. As quoted by the Douglass Archives (douglassarchives.org), he said, "You shall not press down upon the brow of labor this crown of thorns, you shall not crucify mankind upon this cross of gold." The convention went wild and named Bryan its presidential nominee.

Exit the Populists. With their primary issue stolen, they supported Bryan, too. He lost to William McKinley, and, by early 1900, the Populists were absorbed by the Progressives.

THE PROGRESSIVE PARTY

The Progressive Party split from the Republicans to support former president Theodore Roosevelt in the brutal campaign of 1912. Roosevelt had handpicked William Howard Taft to succeed him four years earlier. According to David Gruber's "TR: The Story of Theodore Roosevelt" in PBS's American Experience series, the hands-on Federalist Roosevelt once said, "The President has the legal right to do whatever the needs of the people demand." When Taft did not follow through on his predecessor's reforms, Roosevelt decided that he wanted the presidency back.

Gruber described how politicians reacted when Roosevelt unveiled "New Nationalism," a plan that called for "far more governmental interference in social and economic conditions." Horrified, conservative Republican politicians backed Taft for reelection, pitting Republicans against Republicans. According to Gruber, Roosevelt, who had once called Taft a "big, generous, high-minded fellow," now described his former friend as a "fathead with brains less than a guinea pig." In turn, Taft called Roosevelt a "dangerous egotist, a demagogue, a man who can't tell the truth."

To win the nomination, Roosevelt needed 540 of 1,078 delegates. In states in which the people chose their preferred candidate, Roosevelt won 278 delegates; Taft won 48. Of 12 states with direct primaries, Roosevelt won 9. Taft won states in which conventions and caucuses (controlled by politicians in state legislatures) chose the candidates. Only the police kept the two sides from coming to blows.

At the Republicans' June convention, barbed wire, hidden under bunting, enclosed the speaker's podium to keep the convention chairman safe. The Republican National Committee (controlled by Taft men) awarded Taft 235 of 254 contested delegate seats. In his book *The Bull Moose Years: Theodore Roosevelt and the Progressive Party,* John Gable, another Roosevelt historian, described how delegates reacted to the news: Tempers flared. Men shouted, "Swindler," "Robber," and "We Want Teddy" from the convention floor, and 344 Roosevelt delegates exited the hall. The next day, the *Chicago Tribune* ran a banner headline that read, "THOU SHALT NOT STEAL."

Five weeks later, representatives of the new Progressive Party met in Chicago. Delegates sang "Onward Christian Soldiers" and the "Battle Hymn of the Republic." When Roosevelt took the platform, spectators waved red bandanas, and delegates marched in the aisles for over an

BREAKER BOYS

* * * * *

Although concern for child labor began as early as 1832, families desperate to buy food sent their children into glass factories, textile mills, canneries, and mines. Boys as young as seven, eight, and nine years old were forced to work as breakers above the coal mines where their fathers worked.

Coal, taken from the mine, needed to be sorted and shaped for market. After a huge drum broke off the odd edges, the crushed coal traveled in chutes through the factory to wagons or freight cars outside.

Sitting on boards above the chutes, breaker boys hunched over for 10 to 14 hours a day, grabbing at rock or pieces of slate with bare hands. Overseers watched them, hitting them on the head and shoulders with sticks or bullwhips if they were not working fast enough. The coal dust was so thick that they sometimes wore miners' lamps just to see their hands. The dust blackened their faces, settling on their skin and in their hair. Periodically, they would have to have a doctor clean out the dust that clogged their ears.

hour. Gable wrote that Roosevelt called the new party "a contract with the people" and said that its first principle was "the right of the people to rule." That included women voting, the direct election of senators, and a national primary. He wanted a minimum wage, a commission for mine and factory inspections, workmen's compensation laws, child labor laws, and a mandatory six-day work week. He wanted a public health department and free access to

Heat that was intended to warm the breaker boy room from November to May was often diverted underground for the miners, and the boys were left to fend for themselves, bundling up in overcoats and hats. Because mittens and gloves would get caught on the machinery, their hands were bare. By the end of their daily shift, breaker boys' hands were red and their fingertips were cut and bleeding from sharp coal edges. For their misery, they earned 40 cents a day. After working for four years, they might get up to 90 cents a day.

Today, child labor laws say that the minimum work age is 14 years old, with the exception of newspaper delivery, performing in media or theater productions, and work for parents in nonfarm businesses. A 14-year-old can work a maximum 3 hours per day and 18 hours per week during school and 8 hours per day and 40 hours per week when school is not in session. The work day may begin at 7 A.M. and must conclude before 7 P.M.

mega corporations' records, as well as the elimination of unfair treatment of competitors.

He wanted a strong army and navy, as well, but environmental conservation was his biggest concern. "There can be no greater issue than that of conservation," he said, according to Gable's book. "Grazing lands, forests, and soil, and mineral resources should be preserved."

A famous story that David C. Saffell recounted in *The Encyclopedia of U.S. Presidential Elections* explains how Roosevelt's Progressive Party got its nickname: When reporters asked Roosevelt how he felt, he responded, "fit as a bull moose." Thus, the Progressive Party became the Bull Moose Party. Later, while campaigning in Milwaukee, Roosevelt was shot by a would-be assassin. His steel glasses case stopped the bullet, and he insisted on giving his scheduled speech. According to Saffell's book, he told the astonished crowd, "It takes more than a bullet to kill a Bull Moose." More philosophically, he said, "I believe that the Progressive movement is for making life a little easier for all our people; a movement to take the burdens off the men, and especially the women and children of this country."

Roosevelt's popularity overwhelmed Taft, and Grubin's documentary reported what the other candidates said: "There are so many people in the country who don't like me," Taft commented. The Democratic candidate, Woodrow Wilson, acknowledged Roosevelt's magnetism. "Roosevelt appeals to their imagination," said the cool, restrained politician. "I do not." Comparing them to musical instruments, one historian who appeared on Grubin's PBS program said that "Wilson would be a violin, and Roosevelt is a ukulele."

Even with 4.1 million votes (27 percent), Roosevelt lost. "There is no possibility whatsoever that the Progressive Party could actually win the election," said historian William Harbaugh on the same program. "It's simply inconceivable that on its first run, a third party could have polled enough votes." Instead, it split the Republican vote, giving Wilson the White House. The party disintegrated, and most members drifted back to the Republican fold.

5

Uncle Sam, Can You Spare a Dime?

During frontier days, whiskey was "the good creature of God." According to Thomas Lennon's documentary "Demon Rum," by 1827 it had become "a greater curse than yellow fever," of great concern to many Americans.

PROHIBITION PARTY
The Prohibition Party had cause to organize. Aware of the many Irish and German liquor-drinking voters, the major parties were not interested in banning alcohol, and existing prohibition laws were not enforced.

According to Kruschke's *Encyclopedia of Third Parties in the United States,* the Prohibitionists' 1872 platform "invited all persons, whether total abstainers or not, who recognize the terrible injuries inflicted by the liquor traffic, to unite with us for its overthrow, and to secure thereby peace, order and the protection of persons and property."

Prohibition candidates in 1872, 1876, and 1880 received few votes. Then, other organizations began to support the cause: The Anti-Saloon League and the Woman's Christian Temperance Union believed that, without liquor, crime and corruption would cease, taxpayer money would not have to go to prisons and poorhouses, and corrupt politicians would disappear.

A man who was interviewed for Lennon's "Demon Rum" said, "Take the immigrant and make him American. Take the worker and make him middle class. Take the family and make it whole. This was the compelling dream of prohibition and became the most popular reform of the day."

People increasingly began to support Prohibition. Industrialists like Henry Ford linked poor worker productivity to alcohol. As the United States edged toward war with Germany, others said that Prohibition was patriotic, as many breweries were owned by German Americans. Still others thought that grain should be used for alcohol and to make bread for soldiers.

When the Eighteenth Amendment to the Constitution banned alcohol nationwide in December 1917, disaster

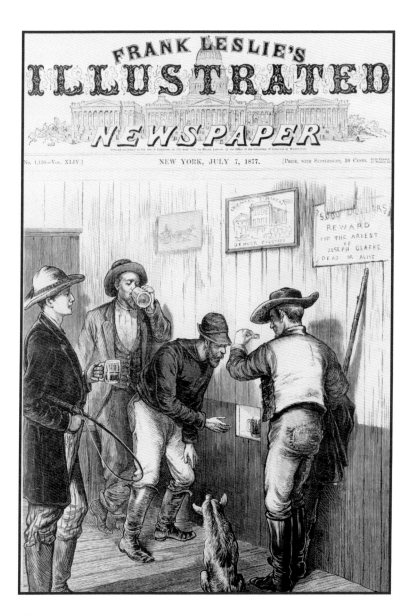

Although nationwide prohibition of alcohol would not take place until 1920 with the passage of the Eighteenth Amendment, individual states or communities had the power to ban alcohol before then. The illustration above, from 1877, shows men disobeying the law in Colorado.

followed. People simply obtained their alcohol illegally. Ten million gallons annually came from Canada, and America brewed even more. Drinkers visited underground nightclubs called "blind pigs" or "speakeasies." They wrangled prescriptions for "medicinal" whiskey from physicians. Patent medicines became another alcohol source.

The result of Prohibition was simply a new set of problems. At first, bootleggers were locals who liked to smuggle a case of whiskey for 50 dollars instead of working for 5 dollars in daily wages. Then, organized crime, like the Purple Gang and the Black Hand, stepped in. Homicides, burglaries, and assaults increased, and bribery of politicians and police was common. Al Capone operated from Chicago, where 400 gang-related murders occurred each year. Half of the police force was on his payroll. Federal agents, never numbering more than 2,500, were overwhelmed. Police often broke into homes to look for alcohol without search warrants, and people were questioned without a reason. Worst yet, children, whom Prohibition was supposed to protect, were touched by crime: "These kids couldn't believe that their fathers would sneak drinks and break the law," said "Red" Cole on Lennon's "Demon Rum." "It made a kid think 'I don't think so very much of the United States's laws.'" Schools even closed campuses to keep bootleggers from approaching students to work for them.

Those who once promoted Prohibition to save the family soon wanted to repeal it for the same reason. Repeal also became an economic issue: Desperate for work in the

Depression, people thought that breweries and saloons would provide jobs and tax revenue. Prohibition thus also became a political issue. Lennon's "Demon Rum" showed

PATENT MEDICINES

The Eighteenth Amendment banned alcohol, and the Volstead Act defined intoxicating liquor as any beverage with greater than 0.5 percent alcohol by volume. It made beer (which was only 3 to 8 percent alcohol) and wine (which was 11 to 12 percent alcohol) illegal. Some people turned to patent medicines for their alcohol fix.

Manufacturers and small family businesses made these secret formula medicines to advertise cures for both common and uncommon ailments. Foley's Honey and Tar supposedly helped colds and coughs. Dr. Miller's Vegetable Expectorate supposedly cured lung problems, and Munson's Paw-Paw Pills supposedly helped liver function. Others claimed to cure cancer, arthritis, baldness, small breasts, and headaches.

Beyond their cure-all claims, these medicines appealed to drinkers because of their alcohol content. Burdock's Tonic Compound contained 10 percent alcohol. Lydia E. Pinkham's Vegetable Compound was advertised to help female troubles. It contained 15 to 20 percent alcohol. Cardui, another medicine for menstruation, backache, and headaches, was 19 percent alcohol. Dr. Hostetter's Stomach Bitters had more than 44 percent alcohol content (more than whiskey, gin, vodka, or rum). No wonder those who took these medicines felt no pain.

Franklin Delano Roosevelt addressing the Democrats in 1932. He said, "This convention wants repeal. Your candidate wants repeal. I am confident that the United States of America wants repeal."

After 16 years, on December 5, 1933, the Twenty-first Amendment repealed Prohibition. The Prohibition Party survived both Prohibition and its repeal because it also supported other vote-getting issues. It backed the right to vote regardless of race or sex; direct election of the president, vice president, and senators; and equal wages regardless of sex. It proposed government control of railroads and telegraphs, revised immigration laws, and pensions for Civil War veterans. The party opposed entering World War I, proposing that soldiers build highways instead. It also wanted free public education, prison reform, and outlawed gambling. The longest-running third party, the Prohibition Party survives—just barely. In the 2004 presidential election, its candidate received only 1,896 votes.

At that time, however, liquor was the least of America's troubles. On October 29, 1929, the stock market collapsed and 30 billion dollars simply disappeared. In the decade that followed, almost half of the country's 25,000 banks closed, and 40 million people were unemployed. In Detroit, one person died of starvation every seven hours. According to the Herbert Hoover Presidential Library, New York hotel clerks asked guests checking in, "Do you want a room for sleeping or for jumping?" To make matters worse, drought withered farmland:

During the Great Depression, many political parties were formed to urge a political solution to the economic problem. Many people were so poor at the time that they were forced to live in shantytowns like the one above, outside of Seattle, Washington.

250 million acres of land lost its topsoil to the "black blizzards" that blew across America's heartland.

Many looked to the government for help, but President Herbert Hoover was no Federalist. He believed that the government should not intervene directly in people's lives. He loaned money to banks and corporations, believing that assistance at the top would create jobs at the bottom, and he asked state and local governments and charities such as the Red Cross to assist the homeless. He would not authorize direct aid, though, and many citizens felt betrayed.

In their documentary "The Crash of 1929" for PBS's American Experience series, Ellen Hovde and Mufie Meyer cited a letter from a war veteran who said,

> *To say that people are not suffering from hunger and actually starving in Arkansas is a blind denial of plain facts. The Red Cross and the states have not the resources. . . . I am utterly disgusted that . . . my national government should shirk its inescapable duty in this time of peril.*

THE LIBERTY PARTY AND THE JOBLESS PARTY

Two small third parties organized to suggest that the federal government act to help the people. The Liberty Party wanted the government to seize basic industries and expand relief projects for the poor. It also wanted additional public works projects to create jobs. On the ballot in only nine states, the Liberty Party received 53,425 votes in 1932. Like many third parties, it lacked campaign funds.

"Pastor of the Poor" Father James Cox led 25,000 unemployed workers to Washington in January 1932. Having failed to pressure Congress into creating a public works program, he formed the Jobless Party. This party proposed that the federal government take over banks, confiscate private wealth, create public works for new jobs, and organize relief programs. Without enough finances, Cox, the party's presidential nominee, withdrew from the campaign the day before the election. He received 740 votes.

BERLIN AIRLIFT AND OPERATION LITTLE VITTLES

During World War II (1939–1945), Berlin was located deep inside the Soviet-held section of Germany. After World War II, it was divided into East Berlin and West Berlin. On June 24, 1948, the Soviets blocked railroad and street access to West Berlin (occupied by American, French, and British troops), denying access to routes that crossed Soviet-occupied Germany. The Soviets also shut off electricity to West Berlin. Such actions revealed Stalin's treacherous plans to take over the world.

Rather than risk war with a display of troops, U.S. planes, nicknamed Rosinenbombers (raisin bombers), airlifted supplies into West Berlin for 462 days from 1948 to 1949. These airlifts delivered 2,326,406 tons of food and supplies including 1.5 million tons of coal. During one period, planes landed at Berlin airports every minute. Planes also dropped tiny handmade parachutes with candy bars and bubble gum for the children of Berlin. That project was named Operation Little Vittles. The British version of the airlift was called Operation Plainfare.

Although the Jobless Party did not survive, its ideas did. Some were eventually incorporated into Franklin Roosevelt's "New Deal." Father Cox continued to work among the poor and was appointed by Roosevelt to serve on the National Recovery Administration.

THE UNION PARTY

The Union Party, or National Union of Social Justice, wanted the federal government completely involved in people's lives. It proposed set annual wages for laborers, a guaranteed profit for farmers, and a guaranteed pension for senior citizens. It wanted Congress to protect small industries from monopolies and wanted federal works to conserve public lands, water, and forests. The party also wanted a limit on the annual income that an individual could make—but it didn't say how, if property taxes were eliminated, the government would fund these programs.

The party was established in 1936 by Reverend Charles E. Coughlin, William Lemke, and Francis Townsend. Thirty million listeners in the United States and Europe heard Coughlin's radio harangues. He wanted social justice for the poor and attacked international banking, Communism, President Roosevelt, and labor unions. Listeners thought that he was either a saint or a Nazi.

Francis Townsend was a champion of the elderly. In 1933, broke and 66 years old, he proposed a $200 monthly federal pension to anyone over 60, on the condition that they spent the money within 30 days. He hoped that this spending would create new jobs. A national sales tax

President Franklin D. Roosevelt established many programs that would create jobs in an effort to combat the Great Depression. Many of these programs led to the construction of public works, such as the Grand Coulee Dam *(above)* in Washington State.

would provide pension funding. Twenty million people signed a petition to support his Old Age Revolving Pension Plan, and two years later, Congress passed the Social Security Act, which is still in force today.

William "Liberty Bell" Lemke headed the ticket. As a U.S. representative, Lemke proposed a bill to protect farmers from losing their property. Roosevelt vetoed it. Lemke wanted revenge, but his 892,492 votes hardly threatened to Roosevelt's 27,751,597. The party fizzled in 1939.

Franklin D. Roosevelt's "New Deal" helped save the country. Legislation prevented banks from foreclosing on farms and helped middle-class homeowners refinance their mortgages. Congress created the Federal Deposit Insurance Corporation (FDIC), which insured deposits up to $5,000. Citizens trusted banks again and used them.

New agencies created jobs. The Civilian Works Administration hired workers to repair roads, parks, and airports, and the Civilian Conservation Corps employed 2.5 million people to maintain and restore natural resources. The Public Works Administration hired 8.5 million for public works projects such as building Grand Coulee Dam.

The government paid farmers not to raise specific crops and to practice conservation techniques such as terracing and contour plowing. The Drought Relief Service bought cattle above market value at $14 to $20 a head, and the Federal Surplus Relief Corporation then fed them to the needy. In 1935, Roosevelt signed the Emergency Relief Appropriations Act, which distributed $525 million. Big government had come to the rescue.

6

RUNNING FROM RED

In a capitalist society, individuals can achieve almost anything. By working hard or by scheming a lot, one person can own an enormous corporation and take all of its profits. In the United States, Cornelius Vanderbilt owned railroads, Andrew Carnegie controlled steel mills, and J.P. Morgan dominated banks. While they raked in billions, their employees barely scraped out a living.

Socialism and communism operate differently, although the two systems have in common their opposition to capitalism. In the socialist belief system, private property and industry do not exist. Workers "collectively" and "cooperatively" control factories, equipment, raw materials, and fuel, and wealth is equally divided.

Under communism, governments own and control everything, distributing wealth to individuals as they please.
The path to communism is through revolution.

Supporters of both philosophies founded third parties
in the United States. During hard times, they appealed to
workers who struggled to support their families.

THE SOCIALIST PARTY

In 1894, Eugene V. Debs and 50,000 sympathetic American Railway Union workers across the nation went on
strike to protest the low wages that George Pullman paid
and the high rent he charged his employees. Rail traffic
stopped. The strike turned violent when President Cleve-
land sent in federal troops. In Chicago, 13 strikers were
killed, 57 were wounded, and property damage totaled
$80 million. Debs and 3 union leaders were arrested.

In jail, Debs read the writings of Karl Marx. He clearly
identified with the socialist working man. Howard Zinn's
"Eugene V. Debs and the Idea of Socialism" is one of
many articles that include Debs's most famous statement:
"While there is a lower class, I am in it. While there is
a criminal element, I am of it. While there is a soul in
prison, I am not free."

Socialists wanted the government turned over to the
working man and public ownership of industries, gold, silver, copper, lead, iron, coal, oil, and gas. They wanted the
cost of living reduced and a shorter work day, and they opposed child labor. The Socialists wanted direct election of
the president and vice president and to abolish the Senate,

THE EMPIRE BUILDERS
" Those Christian men to whom God in his infinite wisdom has given control of the property interests of the country "

In the United States, the "Empire Builders" were men who built economic empires, usually by focusing on a single industry. Second from left is Andrew Carnegie; Cornelius Vanderbilt is third from left; and J.P. Morgan is third from right.

the presidential veto, federal district courts, and courts of appeal. In 1900, Debs ran as their presidential candidate. He ran again in 1904, 1908, 1912, and 1920.

The Socialists were pacifists. They called for eliminating the president's power to declare war and the repeal of laws that authorized funds for the military. In 1918, Debs made an antiwar speech that denounced the draft. He was convicted of interfering with the mail under the Espionage Act of 1917, sentenced to 10 years in prison, and stripped of his American citizenship.

In 1920, Debs ran for president from prison. He attacked the government for undercutting civil liberty, deporting political radicals, and censoring the press, and he wanted to dissolve the League of Nations. Debs lost to Warren G. Harding, but Prisoner 9653 received a surprising 913,664 votes. Harding pardoned Debs the next year. After Debs's death 5 years later, the party nominated Norman Thomas, who headed the Socialist ticket for the next 25 years.

Kruschke's *Encyclopedia of Third Parties in the United States* reported that the Socialist platform claimed, "The best of what goes by the New Deal name—social insurance, minimum wage laws, guarantees of the right to collective bargaining, public power projects—were first demanded by the Socialist Party."

THE COMMUNIST PARTY

Today's Communist Party of the United States of America (CPUSA) resembles an ordinary political organization. It wants a $12 per hour minimum wage, universal insurance and health care, increased taxes on the rich and corporations, public ownership of utilities, a reduced military budget, election reform, and an instant runoff voting procedure. This party is different, however, because it believes that capitalism is America's great evil and proposes to replace it with socialism. The key word is "replace." The

Eugene Debs, a member of the American Socialist Party, ran
as the party's candidate for president five times from 1900
to 1920, the last time from prison.

article "Program of the Communist Party USA" (at http://
www.cpusa.org/article/static/758/) demonstrated that the
CPUSA carefully avoids violent or revolutionary terms,
advising the working class to start a "transformation
to socialism."

The Land of the Free tolerates the Socialist Party as a
third party, but it is not sure about the Communist Party.
Shortly after the party organized in 1919, government
agents undertook the "Palmer Raids," arresting and deporting Communists. Anti-Communist sentiment spread,
and one young radical in Washington was hanged. The
coroner's report, according to Wikipedia's entry on the
Palmer Raids, stated that the Communist "jumped off
with a rope around his neck and then shot himself full
of holes."

Later, the country was friendlier. During the Depression, overthrowing the government appealed to penniless
laborers who lived in cardboard boxes. In 1932, voters
cast 102,991 ballots for the Communist Party. When the
United States and the Soviet Union soldiered together
during World War II, Communist Party membership grew
to between 80,000 and 100,000.

At the war's end, another red scare surfaced. People
realized that the Soviet Union was gobbling up countries
and feared that Communism would soon control the
world. According to Michael Ushan's book *The 1940s*, in
1947, President Harry Truman created the Truman Doctrine, pledging "to confront the Russians with unalterable
counter force at every point where they show signs of

encroaching upon the interests of a peaceful and stable world." Thus, the world split into Communist versus democratic countries.

In 1948, 12 Communist Party officials were convicted under the Alien Registration Act. According to an Internet article (at www.spartacus.schoolnet.co.uk/USAcommunist.htm), it was illegal "to advocate, abet, or teach the desirability of overthrowing the government." These officials were sentenced to five years in prison.

CIVIL RIGHTS

★ ★ ★ ★ ★

During World War II, a million African Americans served in a segregated armed forces. Realizing that Congress would never pass a bill to rectify this, President Harry Truman formally signed an executive order to integrate the military on June 26, 1948. Truman's crusade to end segregation began in 1946, after a black World War II veteran was attacked and blinded by a South Carolina policeman and two other black veterans and their families were killed by a white mob in Georgia.

Two years before that, a black army lieutenant was ordered by a civilian bus driver in Fort Hood, Texas, to get to the back of the bus, "where the colored people belong."* He was a member of the all-black U.S. 761st Tank Battalion. The unit, known as the Black Panthers, had a motto: "Come out fighting." The young soldier was court martialed for insubordination but was eventually acquitted and received an honorable discharge. That man was Jackie Robinson.

Senator Joseph McCarthy's anti-Communist crusade reduced party ranks to 10,000 in the 1950s.

THE PROGRESSIVE PARTY OF 1948

Just hinting that a person was a "Commie" could ruin a political career. In 1948, the Progressive Party formed around Henry A. Wallace. Most of its members were liberals, many were Democrats, and a few were Communists. The association with the last group destroyed Wallace.

Three years later, in 1947, Robinson would break the color barrier by joining the Brooklyn Dodgers baseball team. The team owner, Branch Rickey, handpicked Robinson to integrate the Major Leagues, asking him not to fight back no matter what teammates, opposing teams, umpires, or fans might say—not to fight except with his bat and glove.

Robinson did just that. He ended his rookie season with a .297 batting average and stole 29 bases. His 10-year career included the Rookie of the Year award, National League All Star designation six times, and six pennant-winning Dodger seasons. He was elected to the Baseball Hall of Fame in 1962, his first year of eligibility. His uniform number, 42, was retired from all baseball teams. April 15 is designated Jackie Robinson Day in all major league ballparks.

---

*Isserman, Maurice, and Michael Kazin. *America Divided: The Civil War of the 1960s*. New York: Oxford University Press, 2000, p. 23.

Wallace was a hard-working, effective politician who had become Roosevelt's third-term vice president. With Roosevelt's health failing, Democratic conservatives realized that Wallace, a liberal, might become president. They convinced Roosevelt to replace Wallace with Harry Truman and to make Wallace secretary of commerce.

When Roosevelt died, Truman inherited his cabinet, including Wallace. Wallace had traveled to Russia in 1944 for Roosevelt and saw that the Soviets were studying atomic energy. Believing that the USSR would soon master it anyway, he suggested that the United States build friendly relations by offering information. Truman could not understand Henry Wallace's sympathetic attitude and fired him.

The Progressive Party opposed the Cold War, the Truman Doctrine, the Marshall Plan, development of more military bases, military training, and military aid. It favored disarmament with Russia and the United Nations's becoming the world government. It supported a minimum wage, old-age pensions, cabinet departments for culture and education, and wanted to abolish the House Committee on Un-American Activities. The party also wanted 18-year-olds to have the right to vote.

The Progressives hated segregation. The platform advocated full voting rights for blacks. Unusual in his time, Henry Wallace refused to appear before segregated audiences or to eat or stay in segregated establishments.

Wallace fell victim to the Red Scare. Almost immediately, he was attacked as anti-American, if not pro-Communist.

Henry Wallace, a member of the Progressive Party, is shown as he delivers a campaign speech at a black church in Knoxville, Tennessee. Wallace was unusual for his time because he refused to speak in front of audiences that were segregated by race.

The press rarely reported his anti-Communist remarks, and he refused to publicly disavow Communism or clarify his beliefs. Communists in the Progressive Party were allowed to stay, and when the Communist Party endorsed Wallace, his career died. He received only 1,157,140 votes from 45 states. The Progressive Party disbanded in 1955, when anti-Communism dominated politics.

THE LIBERAL PARTY

The Liberal Party, a small third party, operates mostly in New York. Formed in 1944, it endorses and supports major party candidates instead of naming its own. Labor groups and intellectuals from the left support it. In 1948, it opposed Henry Wallace, pulling liberal voters from the Progressives, and worked hard for Truman's reelection. Because Wallace's Progressives deserted over foreign policy and Southern states exited over civil rights, Truman did not seem likely to win. Surprisingly, in a low voter turnout, Truman won. Once again, a third party that did not win votes in large numbers affected an election.

THE POOR MAN'S PARTY

The Poor Man's Party was organized in 1952 by Henry Krajewski, a pig farmer. Kruschke's *Encyclopedia of Third Parties in the United States* described how Krajewski campaigned: He carried a black and white pig under his arm to symbolize the squealing of the American people from government "hogging."

This short-lived party wanted lower taxes, a strong defense, victory in the Korean War, and the annexation of Canada. It refused to recognize Communist China and wanted every young American to work on a farm for one year. It also favored a two-president system whereby a Republican and a Democrat would watchdog each other. Krajewski received 4,000 votes for president in 1952 and in 1956 received more than 35,000 votes when he ran for a New Jersey Senate seat. The Poor Man's Party died with him in 1960.

THE CONSTITUTION PARTY

The very conservative Constitution Party was also created in 1952 and survived through five elections. The party wanted restricted federal power, especially in civil rights legislation, and reduced welfare programs. It favored rigid immigration regulations and wanted a balanced federal budget, tax cuts, and increased military spending—all at the same time. Its hot-button issues included the right to pray in public schools, U.S. withdrawal from the United Nations, and refusal to recognize Communist governments. The Constitution Party appeared on nine states' ballots. In 1968, its presidential and vice-presidential candidates received only 34 votes in North Dakota.

There is a current Constitution Party, founded in the 1990s, that is active today, but it is not related to the party of the 1950s and 1960s.

7

"THAT DAY IS JUST GONE"

Although the Civil War had ended long ago, civil rights were still a controversial issue. In 1948, the lines between black and white were clearly marked.

That year, the Democratic Party splintered like a dry log. Henry Wallace's Progressives exited over foreign policy, particularly that concerning Soviet Russia, and Southern Democrats bolted over the old argument between the federal government and states rights. Simply put, the "Dixiecrats" wanted segregation; their president did not.

Truman, a Democrat, wanted to integrate the military and establish fair employment practices for federal civil service agencies. His supporters wanted the abolition of poll taxes, a federal antilynching law, desegregation legislation, and a permanent committee to prevent discrimination in federally funded jobs.

At the Democratic convention, Hubert Humphrey passionately pushed the civil rights plank forward. In his speech, he courageously declared:

> To those who say . . . that we are rushing this issue of civil rights, I say to them we are 172 years too late! . . . To those who say that this civil rights program is an infringement on states' rights, I say this: the time has arrived in America for the Democratic Party to get out of the shadow of states' rights and walk forthrightly into the bright sunshine of human rights!

STATES' RIGHTS PARTY OR DIXIECRATS

Outraged, Mississippi and Alabama delegates left the convention and organized the States' Rights Party. They blustered about maintaining balance between federal government and state government. According to Kruschke's *Encyclopedia of Third Parties in the United States,* however, their platform supported "the racial integrity of each race," and "the constitutional right to choose one's associates." Its campaign motto was "Segregation Forever!"

Headed by South Carolina Governor J. Strom Thurmond, the Dixiecrats hoped to throw the election to the House of Representatives. Thurmond received only 1,169,134 votes from Alabama, Louisiana, Mississippi,

Then the governor of South Carolina, Strom Thurmond (in dark suit) campaigned for president as a Dixiecrat. Although his presidential bid was unsuccessful, he went on to have one of the longest-running careers in the U.S. Senate, which he did not leave until he was in his 90s.

and South Carolina, however, carrying just 39 electoral votes. Most Dixiecrats returned to the Democratic Party after the election, but they loosened the Democrats' monopoly on the South and allowed Republican influence.

CHRISTIAN NATIONAL PARTY

Other white racist parties were more extreme. The Christian National Party formed in Eureka Springs, Arkansas, in 1947. Kruschke's *Encyclopedia of Third Parties* reported that Reverend Gerald Lyman Kenneth Smith was called "The Father Coughlin of the South." Smith hated blacks and Jews. He wanted both deported and the United Nations closed. He also called for increased veterans benefits and aid to the elderly and farmers. He netted only 42 votes. Undaunted, he ran in 1952 and 1956, when he received 8 votes out of 52 million cast.

NATIONAL STATES' RIGHTS PARTY

The National States' Rights Party was founded in 1956 by Edward R. Fields. It believed that members were chosen by God to preserve the white race. With chapters in 31 states, party members wanted complete segregation, the deportation of African Americans to Africa, and immigration limited to Caucasians. They wanted officials who supported integration impeached and all Supreme Court Justices given the death penalty. The party supported several segregationist candidates but was most active in inciting riots and bombing black churches and Jewish synagogues. Fields's party newspaper was read by Klansmen and neo-Nazis. Thankfully, the party died in 1987.

AFRICAN-AMERICAN PARTY

Across the color line, other third parties ranged from the moderate to the extreme. The African-American Party wanted blacks involved in state and national politics. Believing that Southern Democrats were hard-core

KENT STATE SHOOTINGS

★ ★ ★ ★ ★

On April 20, 1970, President Nixon, who had promised to end the Vietnam War, announced that American troops had invaded neutral Cambodia. Angry and feeling betrayed, students (many of whom faced the possibility of being drafted) protested on 1,000 college campuses.

The violence climaxed at Kent State University in Kent, Ohio, after three days of protests. On Friday, students demonstrated on campus. That night, about 100 drunk bikers, students, and out-of-towners staged a disturbance in town. The mayor asked Ohio's governor to send the National Guard.

On Saturday, about 2,000 students burned down an ROTC building that was already scheduled for demolition. They threw objects at firemen and cut the fire hoses. On Sunday, 700 students gathered together. Guardsmen threw tear gas at them, so the students moved into town, where they staged a sit-in. Guardsmen followed. At 11:00 P.M. they announced a curfew and tried to herd students back to campus. In the scuffle, 10 Guardsmen were hurt; at least one student was bayonetted.

Then, more tragedy struck. On Monday, May 4, 2,000 students gathered in a peaceful demonstration on the campus commons. The Guardsmen, fearing more violence, ordered the crowd to disperse. The students stayed put.

At noon, with orders to break up the crowd, the Guardsmen lobbed tear gas at the students. Students threw rocks and returned some of the tear gas canisters. National Guardsmen advanced on the crowd and then found themselves trapped on a football practice field. As they retreated, followed by students, 29 Guardsmen turned and fired 55 rifle bursts, 5 pistol shots, and a shotgun blast into the crowd.

Thirteen seconds later, four students lay dead and nine more were wounded. Seven had bullets in their sides and four in their backs, indicating that they were running from, not toward, the soldiers. Two of the dead were protesters; the other two had been walking across campus to change classes. The closest body to the Guardsmen was 71 feet away; the farthest was 750 feet. The Guardsmen, however, defended their actions by saying that they were being threatened by "a charging mob."*

The country was stunned. "When I saw the students in their pools of blood, I said, 'This is it, it's got to stop–the protests, the war. It's gone too far,' " said Paul Tople, whose photograph of Mary Ann Vecchio came to symbolize the nation's anguish.**

Colleges, high schools, and elementary schools closed to protest the shooting, affecting 4 to 8 million students. President Nixon's commission to study the tragedy sympathized with neither group. "Students who bomb and burn are criminals," it concluded. "Police and National Guardsmen who needlessly shoot or assault students are criminals. All who applaud these criminal acts share in the evil."***

No one applauded either the Kent State shootings or the Vietnam War, which contributed to them.

---

*Isserman, Maurice, and Michael Kazin. *America Divided: The Civil War of the 1960s.* New York: Oxford University Press, 2000, p. 7.
**Kent State shootings remembered. http://archives.cnn.com/2000/US/05/04/kent.state.revisit/.
***Ibid., p. 8.

segregationists, they thought that nothing would be accomplished unless blacks formed their own party. Created in 1960, the party nominated presidential and vice presidential candidates, but they received less than 1,500 votes. With Congress passing civil rights legislation and the Democratic Party courting African-American support, the party lost its issue and disappeared before the next election.

FREEDOM NOW PARTY

The Freedom Now Party was another African-American party. Its candidates in New York, Connecticut, and California were defeated. In 1964, it ran 39 black candidates in Michigan. Again, its dismal failure emphasized that a third party focused on race could not succeed.

MISSISSIPPI FREEDOM DEMOCRATIC PARTY

In 1962, with only 6.7 percent of its African Americans registered, Mississippi's voting record was the worst in the country. In 1963, civil rights activists worked there in a summer-long voter registration drive. At the center of "Freedom Summer" was the Mississippi Freedom Democratic Party (MFDP), a splinter third party of 80,000 Mississippians. Formed in April 1964, it challenged the all-white Mississippi delegation to the Democratic National Convention in August. This "official" all-white delegation had two liabilities: First, it would not support President Lyndon Johnson, whose administration had

The Mississippi Freedom Democratic Party formed as a challenge to the all-white Mississippi delegation to the Democratic National Convention in 1962. Fannie Lou Hamer, above, ran as an MFDP congressional candidate.

pushed civil rights legislation. Second, African Americans had not participated in electing it.

The MFDP elected 64 of its own delegates and headed to Atlantic City, New Jersey, but Johnson did not want a nasty racial confrontation within the party instead of celebrating his progress in civil rights. At the convention, the MFDP argued that its delegation should be seated, and white delegations threatened to walk out.

The story of what happened next was recorded in the Internet article "Mississippi Freedom Democratic Party (MFDP)" (at http://users.skynet.be/suffrage-universal/us/uspamfdp.htm): The MFDP appealed to the Democrats' Credentials Committee. Martin Luther King Jr., James Farmer, and Roy Wilkins testified. An MFDP congressional candidate, Fannie Lou Hamer, described the threats and beatings she suffered while trying to register to vote. Facing television cameras, she asked, "Is this America, the land of the free and the home of the brave, where we are threatened daily because we want to live as decent human beings?" Embarrassed by the bad publicity, the convention proposed a compromise: The all-white delegation would represent Mississippi if it promised to support Johnson during the balloting. The MFDP chairman and national committeeman would be given seats on the floor as nonvoting delegates-at-large. The convention promised to integrate the delegates by 1968.

The MFDP was insulted. "Now, Lyndon made the typical white man's mistake," said one MFDP delegate, also quoted in the article "Mississippi Freedom Democratic

Party." "Not only did he say, 'you've got two votes,' which was too little, but he told us to whom the two votes would go. . . . This is typical white man picking black folks' leader, and that day is just gone."

In one way, the controversy had been a waste of time. Only three of the white delegates would sign the loyalty pledge; the rest left. Johnson was nominated by acclamation, so delegates did not vote individually. In another way, though, the MFDP focused national attention on Mississippi's voting practices—or lack of them.

The MFDP continued work to obtain more voting rights for African Americans and helped elect more black office-holders in Mississippi than in any other state. In 1968, its members were included in the "official" delegation to the Democratic Party convention in Chicago.

BLACK PANTHERS

Others, dismayed at the outcome, turned militant. One group was the Black Panthers. The Black Panther Party organized in October 1966. Originally called the Black Panther Party for Self-Defense, it maintained that blacks had a right to defend themselves by any means necessary. It formed neighborhood patrols, monitored police, and protected people against police brutality. The Panthers nicknamed the police "pigs."

The Panther platform demanded that the federal government give full employment to blacks and take housing from white landlords and give it to the black community. It proposed that black men be excused from military

Eldridge Cleaver, in sunglasses, stands with other members of the Black Panthers (*above*). Cleaver ran as the Peace and Freedom Party presidential nominee in 1968.

service and freed from jail and that black juries judge black defendants. In May 1967, fully armed Panthers marched on the California state capital to protest pending legislation that would ban carrying loaded weapons in public.

During the next five years, Black Panthers and police often clashed, with casualties on both sides. Their most violent exchange occurred in 1969, when, according to Panthers, Chicago police broke into an apartment without reason and shot two members in their sleep. The fact that many Black Panther convictions were later overturned indicates that this group may have been unduly targeted by the police.

At its peak in the late 1960s, Panther membership increased to 2,000, with chapters in several cities. The party lost its prominence as its leaders disagreed and left, and differing philosophies within the group weakened it as well.

In 1973, perhaps because other black leaders did not support its activities, the Black Panther Party turned away from violence and began to emphasize community programs such as free breakfasts for school children, free health clinics, special education classes, free food and clothing, and drives against drug abuse.

Eldridge Cleaver, a Black Panther minister of defense, ran as the Peace and Freedom Party presidential nominee in 1968. Later, he was wounded in a police shoot-out, jumped bail, and fled to Algeria, France, and Cuba. In later years, he became a born-again Christian and ran unsuccessfully as a Republican candidate for a California Senate seat.

8

GIVE PEACE
A CHANCE

Vietnam was a country split in half. Between 1954 and 1975, the Communists of North Vietnam (supported by China and the Soviet Union) fought non-Communist South Vietnam (supported by the United States).

Determined to stop Communists from taking over Vietnam's southern half, the United States first sent military advisers to help the South Vietnamese fight the Communist Viet Cong. Starting at 900 in 1960, the number of advisers soon increased to 11,000. By 1965, 170,000 American soldiers were in combat. Three years later, 500,000 troops occupied Vietnam.

The American armed forces were accustomed to winning. Politicians decided that this war would not be fought to win but to contain Communism. American soldiers were used to traditional warfare, using guns, bombs, and tanks, but the Viet Cong ambushed their enemy and then faded into the jungle. At home, President Johnson claimed that the United States was winning. When the Viet Cong attacked 36 cities in the Tet Offensive, though, the public questioned the president's decisions and honesty. U.S. servicemen became depressed—they no longer believed that what they were fighting for was a just cause. In *The Vietnam War,* Roger Barr quoted a soldier: "I felt no sense of accomplishment other than my friends and I had helped each other to survive. We didn't act to help our country, but to save our buddies."

PEACE AND FREEDOM PARTY

Third parties sprang up in protest. The Peace and Freedom Party organized in 1967 to give voice to those who were unhappy with the situation in Vietnam, labor unions, racism, and sexism. It called for U.S. military withdrawal and wanted a socialist economy in which industries, finances, and natural resources were owned and managed by the people. In 1968, Black Panther Eldridge Cleaver, at the time a convicted felon, was chosen over Dick Gregory as its presidential nominee. The party's candidates appeared in 19 states, tallied 136,385 popular votes, and received no electoral votes. The party ran presidential candidates until 2004 and today operates primarily in California. This party wants a guaranteed income, a 30-hour workweek for 40 hours' pay, and a required annual 4-week paid vacation. The Peace and Freedom Party wants both

Above, a truckload of Vietnam War protestors arrives to join an estimated 60,000 people attending a rally in protest of U.S. involvement in the war on April 15, 1967. That year, the Peace and Freedom Party was founded.

Spanish and English as official languages of California and supports open borders and full political, social, and economic rights for resident noncitizens.

FREEDOM AND PEACE PARTY

The Freedom and Peace Party broke off from the Peace and Freedom Party in 1968 to support Dick Gregory's write-in candidacy. An African-American comedian, Gregory was popular with both black and white audiences for poking fun at racial issues. Gerald Nachman quoted one of Gregory's most famous jokes in his book *Seriously Funny:*

The Rebel Comedians of the 1950s and 1960s. Gregory said, "My daughter, she doesn't believe in Santa Claus. She knows doggone well no white man is coming into a colored neighborhood after midnight." Gregory's strong anti–Vietnam War beliefs inspired a 40-day fast in 1967. By drinking only distilled water, Gregory lost most of his bodyweight: He went from 288 pounds to 97.

Gregory and the Freedom and Peace Party's primary causes were the Vietnam War and civil rights. They wanted an end to the war, provisions for families of soldiers killed in the war, expanded welfare and education, and a lowered voting age. They called for investigating conditions on Indian reservations and rural problems, and opposed the sale and manufacture of handguns. Gregory received 47,133 votes in the election. His party inaugurated him as "president in exile" on March 4, 1969.

Elsewhere, antiwar protests rocked university campuses and city streets. Demonstrators staged sit-ins, burned draft cards, and broke into government offices. According to Barr's book, Columbia University students wrote to the North Vietnamese, "We are Americans who are deeply opposed to the U.S. bombing raids against the people of North Vietnam. We are doing all that we can to stop these barbarous attacks."

Senator Eugene McCarthy challenged President Johnson for the Democratic nomination. When McCarthy did well in the primaries, President Johnson announced that he would not seek reelection in 1968. Johnson's vice president, Hubert Humphrey, took the Democratic nomination,

Comedian Dick Gregory spoke to students at the University of South Florida in 1971. Gregory's write-in candidacy was supported by the Freedom and Peace Party in 1968.

but he was plagued by Johnson's poor legacy in Vietnam, and lost to Republican Richard M. Nixon.

Nixon supplied massive aid to the South Vietnamese, and, in 1970, ordered the bombing of neighboring Cambodia and Laos. Antiwar protests on college campuses became uncontrollable.

PEOPLE'S PARTY

In 1971, at the height of the Vietnam War, pediatrician Dr. Benjamin Spock and author Gore Vidal formed the People's Party for socialists, pacifists, and antiwar protesters. According to Kruschke's *Encyclopedia of Third Parties in the United States*, the party's platform declared,

"Since we believe that the present political parties of the United States neither represent nor reflect the political, economic, and social hopes of a large segment of people in this country, we shall unite into a new party for positive change."

The party wanted to halve military spending, eliminate sales and property taxes, and set incomes between $6,500 and $50,000. It called for withdrawal of all American troops from foreign countries and legalizing abortion, marijuana, and homosexuality.

Spock received only 78,751 votes, 55,000 of them from California. In 1972, the People's Party was just too radical for the general public. It survived only through the 1976 election.

After more bloody fighting, the Communists took over South Vietnam on April 30, 1975. Four million Vietnamese civilians and one million Vietnamese soldiers lost their lives; 58,226 U.S. soldiers either died or went missing in action. Humiliated, America realized that it had lost the longest war in its history. Its politicians lost the public's trust.

THE LIBERTARIAN PARTY

A significant third party that survives today was established in 1971. The Libertarian Party believes that the less government—both federal and state—the better. The Libertarian Party home page says in its platform: "We hold that all individuals have the right to exercise sole dominion over their own lives, and have the right to live in whatever manner they choose, so long as they do not forcibly interfere with the equal right of others to live in whatever manner they choose."

Libertarians agree with conservatives on certain economic matters—lowering taxes and reducing bureaucratic regulation of business. They want a gradual elimination of the social security and welfare programs, military withdrawal from other countries, the North Atlantic Treaty Organization (NATO), and the United Nations. Libertarians agree with liberals, though, that people have the right to choose their own lifestyles.

Libertarians oppose the Republican-backed USA PATRIOT Act, which was passed after the terrorist attacks of September 11, 2001. This act permits government or police access to phone, Internet, medical, library, and school records for the purpose of terrorist investigations and allows authorities to enter a suspect's home without his or her knowledge or a search warrant.

The party has had some success. In 1972, Libertarians qualified for two states' ballots. An elector liked them so much that he voted for the Libertarian candidate instead of Richard Nixon, his party's choice. Four years later, the Libertarians nominated the elector for president. By 1980, Libertarians were on all 50 states' ballots, the first time a third party accomplished that since the Socialist Party in 1916. The Libertarian Party has 200,000 members, and 600 of its members hold office.

NATIONAL UNITY PARTY

In 1980, a congressman from Illinois emerged from the election-year clamor. Once a conservative Republican,

John Anderson changed in the 1960s and 1970s. In *The Encyclopedia of Third Parties in America*, Immanuel Ness and James Ciment wrote that Anderson described the Vietnam War as "the most tragic error in diplomacy and military policy in our nation's history" and was the first Republican to call for Nixon's resignation after the Watergate scandal. According to Ness and Ciment, a fellow congressman told Anderson, "You're in the wrong party, John." In 1980, Anderson challenged Ronald Reagan in Republican primaries. Badly beaten, Anderson reappeared as a National Unity Party candidate. Anderson billed himself as the "man in the middle," more liberal than Reagan and more conservative than incumbent President Jimmy Carter. He appealed to young people, women, and gun-control advocates.

Anderson supported a 50-cent per gallon tax on gas for social security funding and tax cuts for businesses, and he opposed defense spending for the M-X missile and the B-1 bomber. These ideas were considered radical, but, like other third party ideas, they later became accepted. Reagan gave tax cuts to businesses, which helped the economy, and the M-X missile and B-1 bomber proved to be budget disasters. Two decades later, politicians have become alarmed at rapidly diminishing social security funds, which Anderson's gas tax might have prevented.

The National Unity Party faced typical third-party obstacles. One was getting on the ballots. Another was finding money. As a representative of a startup organization, Anderson could not receive any federal funding until after the election—and then only if he got 5 percent of the vote.

Carter's funds totaled $54 million, and Reagan topped at $64 million. Reagan's media purchases exceeded Anderson's entire budget.

PRESIDENTIAL DEBATES

Presidential debates began on September 26, 1960, as Vice President Richard M. Nixon and Democratic nominee John F. Kennedy faced off with more than 66 million people watching. Because of the dramatic effect of the debates, candidates in the 1964, 1968, and 1972 campaigns would not appear on television. The debates resumed in 1976, when President Gerald Ford and Democrat Jimmy Carter debated.

The League of Women Voters, a nonpolitical group, sponsored the debates until demands made by both major parties caused it to withdraw. In 1988, the debates were taken over by the Commission on Presidential Debates, which is made up of members of the two major parties. They effectively eliminated third-party candidates from participating by requiring that participants show 15-percent support in the presidential election polls. The only third-party candidates to qualify have been John Anderson (debating only Republican candidate Ronald Reagan) and Ross Perot.

Three or four journalists question the candidates in front of a live audience. The candidates are granted a short opening statement, 90 seconds to answer a question with a 60-second rebuttal, a 30-second response, and a 2-minute closing. The number of viewers varies, topping out at 70 million.

In September, Anderson's candidacy received a boost when the League of Women Voters asked him to participate in the presidential debates. He was the first third-party candidate invited. Ronald Reagan debated him once, but President Carter refused, and Anderson was excluded from two October debates. "It was absolutely crushing," he told a television interviewer on a PBS News-hour program. "I am absolutely convinced that I would have gotten more than double the vote that I did get."

For a third-party candidate, getting to the debate podium with the major candidates is important. As many as 70 million people watch. It also makes a third-party candidate credible. Anderson told the PBS interviewer, "It gives him a legitimacy that makes it possible for him to be a real contender."

Ronald Reagan won the election with 43 million votes; Jimmy Carter received 35 million. Spread evenly across the country, 5.7 million people voted for Anderson.

9

A CLOSE CALL

The question of whether the federal government or the states should have more influence divided America's Founding Fathers into the first two political parties, and today inspires many third parties. More recently, both major parties and third parties have been concerned with whether or not the federal government has become too big or too corrupt to care for the average American. Elections at the end of the 1990s and into the twenty-first century examined these issues.

INDEPENDENT: ROSS PEROT

In 1992, billionaire Ross Perot stepped into the spotlight by criticizing the federal government. He wanted to reduce both its size and its spending of taxpayers' money.

Carmen Bredeson's biography, *Ross Perot: Billionaire Politician,* quoted Perot: "Government is not a candy store in which every group can pick from any jar it wants. This is not free money. It's your money and more importantly, it's your children's money." Disillusioned by the major parties, many believed that Perot was the kind of "go-to guy" who could fix the government's problems.

In high school, he organized a yearbook staff when he discovered that none existed. He even convinced school administrators to buy a larger lot to build a new school. "He had covered every angle," said a teacher quoted in Bredeson's book. "He had maps, graphs, tables, charts—everything." Another teacher, Claude Pinkerton, told him, "You could be president of the United States if you desired." Bredeson reported Perot's answer: "Mr. Pinkerton, that wouldn't be bad, would it?"

In the 1960s, when computers were too new to be much understood, Perot figured out how to process Medicare and Medicaid applications for the government. When his company, Electronic Data Systems, was sold a few years later, Perot became a billionaire.

During the Vietnam War, Perot sent two jets to North Vietnam with food for American POWs. In 1978, two of his employees were kidnapped in Iran and held for $12,750,000 ransom. When American diplomats could not help, Perot hired a commando force that freed them.

On February 20, 1992, Perot announced on "Larry King Live" that he would run for president if the people got his name on every state's ballot. Public support was immediate because Americans were fed up with the politicians in Washington, D.C. In 1992, the national debt was growing by $12,000 a second, and Perot seemed just the man to fix it. "Ross for Boss" and "Run, Ross, Run" T-shirts appeared.

The next months were bizarre. Perot was an experienced businessman but new to politics. When he did not offer specific solutions for the nation's problems, public opinion slipped. The press turned on him, and he withdrew from the race in July. Loyal followers convinced him to come back. Having qualified with 15 percent of polled votes, he was invited to join Democrat Bill Clinton and incumbent President George H.W. Bush in three presidential debates. Viewers liked his shoot-from-the-hip answers. According to Bredeson's biography, when challenged about his inexperience, Perot replied, "They've got a point. I don't have any experience running up a $4 trillion debt."

Perot finally explained his programs. He wanted a 50-cent per gallon gas hike and a 10-percent cost reduction in all government branches. He promised higher cigarette taxes and 10 percent per gallon gasoline tax each year for five years. He wanted the people to vote directly for president instead of going through the Electoral College. He also proposed toll-free phone lines so that citizens could tell the government their opinions and electronic "town hall meetings" so that citizens could vote from home. Perot dipped into his own pocket for $65.4 million in campaign funding and bought television time to speak to the American people. Using charts and graphs like he did in high school, he talked

Ross Perot became one of the most enduring symbols of an independent candidacy when he ran for president in 1992. In part because of his personal wealth, Perot was able to attract a lot of media attention.

about the budget deficit and government overspending in "infomercials."

When the election results were tallied in November, Perot had collected 19,097,215 popular votes but no electoral votes. Perot had run as an independent without any political party for support. In 1995, he organized the Reform Party and ran as its candidate. His 1996 totals were less than half of those in 1992. Some said that his showing was poor because Republican candidate Robert Dole would not allow him into the presidential debates. Others believe the public lost faith in him after the outcome of the previous election. Afterward, Perot rarely spoke on political issues.

In 1998, Jesse Ventura, a former wrestler and Navy demolition SEAL, ran for Minnesota governor on the Reform ticket. Ventura told voters that he was a pragmatic leader rather than a professional politician. After his election, without any Reform Party legislators in the state government, his policies floundered.

In 2000, conservative Pat Buchanan tried a "hostile takeover" of the Reform Party. He eventually wrested the nomination from another hopeful but did not finish well, getting only 400,000 votes. The Reform Party disintegrated soon after that. Most members joined either Buchanan's newly formed America First Party or Ralph Nader in the 2004 election.

RALPH NADER

Ralph Nader has run for president in 1996, 2000, and 2004. The first two times, he was connected to the Green Party. The third time he ran as an independent.

In 2000, the longtime consumer advocate campaigned against corporations. He supported campaign finance reform, environmental justice, universal health care, affordable housing, free education through college, workers' rights, and placing the tax burden more on corporations than on the middle and lower classes. He opposed pollution credits and giveaways of publicly owned assets. His real reason for running, though, was to gain the required

5 percent popular vote that would qualify the Green Party for federal funds in the next election.

Everyone knew that Nader could not win. Many realized, however, that a third party could once again play

EXIT POLLS

Part of the confusion in the 2000 election stemmed from exit poll errors. Exit polls are set up in particular places throughout the country because they supposedly give an idea of how the rest of the state will vote and indicate the final outcome. Besides asking who they voted for, 30,000 interviewers also questioned voters about election issues such as tax cuts and health care for the elderly and took personal information such as age, race, gender, marital status, political party, employment, education, religion, and family income. Based on the information, those who run the exit polls predict a winner.

The Voter News Service was organized and used by ABC, CBS, CNN, FoxNews, NBC, the Associated Press, and 19 newspapers. The nightmare of the 2000 election began when the Voter News Service declared Vice President Al Gore the winner. It gave its projections to the networks and to the AP, who then decided whether or not to make their own election calls. When one network declares a winner, though, the others usually follow—which is exactly what happened. As voting results continued to come in, the Voter News Service changed its mind. The media did, too, and confusion resulted.

"spoiler" to the final outcome. Democrats campaigned against Nader with the old anti–third party argument that a vote for Nader was a wasted vote. They suggested that, because a Nader vote did not count anyway, Nader supporters should vote for the major party candidate who most closely represented their views: Vice President Al Gore. Nader's response was that voters did not "belong" to Gore—or to anyone.

On election night, as vote totals teeter-tottered between them, Gore first called to congratulate Bush on his election, then retracted his concession, and finally called to concede a second time. The election boiled down to who won Florida's electoral votes.

As it turned out, after recounts, legal battles, and a Supreme Court decision, the difference between either Bush or Gore winning Florida (and the presidency) was only 537 votes. Had just a few of Nader's 97,488 votes gone to Gore, he would have been president. Many analysts believe that Nader's presence on the ballot threw the election to the Republicans. Nader supporters said that, if anything was responsible for Gore's loss, it was losing Tennessee's (his own state's) electoral votes. Nader was more philosophical when he spoke to Michael Hastings for the *Newsweek* article "Ralph Nader; Playing the Spoiler Again." Nader said, "Playing 'what if' with the Green Party means Americans should only have a choice between two parties that own the country, and that third parties should get out of the way," said Nader. "That's not acceptable."

The 2004 election was a tangled web of charges and countercharges. Nader entered the race again, still angry with big business control of the two major parties, the poor environmental record of Bush administration, and how the Patriot Act was violating due process.

Democrats were determined that Nader's votes would not influence the final outcome again, and they began "anti-Nader" commercials in important locations. State by state, they took him to court, challenging his right to be on the ballot.

Katherine Seelye's article "Convictions Intact, Nader Soldiers On" quoted a Nader volunteer who helped get signatures on ballot petitions and resented the Democrats' efforts: "My vote is my vote and I'll go where I want to with it," she said. "If they don't keep that door open for a third party, some day the ballot is going to say 'yes or no' and it's going to be one name, and that's my fear if we limit our choice now."

The Green Party, which supported Nader four years before, endorsed its own candidate. Nader then tried to get on ballots as the nominee of Ross Perot's Reform Party.

Nader was anti–Iraq war and anticorporation. He called for a new government health insurance and guaranteed "living wages" for workers. In Scott Shane's *New York Times* article "Nader Is Left With Fewer Votes and Friends, After '04 Race," Nader asked, "What about the morality of corporate crime, the morality of dangerous workplaces and deaths from air pollution and bad hospital practices." Nader wanted to reform the two-party political system by adding a NOTA (None of the Above) line on ballots in case voters did not like any candidate and preferred another election.

In the end, Nader's votes in 34 states totaled only a little over 400,000, down from nearly 3 million in 2000. Despite the decreased number of votes cast, the effort to squash Nader's campaign showed how much the major parties fear what a third party can do.

Nader was not the only third-party candidate in 2004. There were 12 official third parties, 4 independents, and 36 write-in candidates for president. The fact is that, as long as there is a government and any dissatisfaction with the major parties, there will be citizens who want change. These rebels find a voice in forming third parties.

It is an uphill battle. Running a campaign requires millions of dollars, and qualifying for federal funds is a long, complicated process. As a minority, a third party depends on the media. If the media like the third-party issue or if it has a particularly slow news day and something needs to be reported to fill time, a third party might get publicity. The grandest publicity of all is to be included in presidential debates with the other major-party candidates. Millions watch the candidates, and the exposure is free. But if the media do not cover a third party, the party sinks into oblivion.

Despite overwhelming odds, third parties organize anyway. They feel passionately for "the cause." Banding together with like-minded people serves as an outlet for frustrations and gives hope that people are not powerless.

Third parties appear for a multitude of reasons. People get upset with traditional political parties and splinter off from them. Sometimes, they form around a particularly impressive personality. The Bull Moose Party organized for Teddy Roosevelt, the Reform Party existed only to help Ross Perot, and the American Independent Party formed for George Wallace. Take away the personality, as when Wallace was crippled in an assassination attempt, and the party fades. Sometimes, third parties rally around an issue. The Progressives wanted a new money system; the Prohibitionists wanted alcohol banned. If an issue sparks public interest or imagination, though, the major parties are quick to assume the idea themselves. That can destroy third parties or push them into a "me, too" position.

Still, third parties are vital to America's electoral process. They give voice to public concerns that the major parties are reluctant to address. Third parties were the first to speak out against slavery and the first to propose that women have the right to vote. They were the first to propose direct election of public officials and first to ask for a graduated income tax. They were also the first to push for an 18-year-old voting age. Third parties are voices for change, and because of them, our country and our lives are all the better.

GLOSSARY

abolitionists People who wanted to abolish, or get rid of, slavery.

acclamation An oral vote, with great enthusiasm, taken without formality.

aliens People who are not citizens of the country in which they live.

capitalism An economic system based on private and corporate ownership.

concede To admit or yield.

conservative A person who wants to keep everything the same and is suspicious of change; usually believes that the less government interference, the better.

cooperative (co-op) A business that is owned and operated by a group for its members' benefit.

draft To select an individual from a group for some compulsory activity, usually military service.

demagogue A leader who gains power by appealing to the prejudices and emotions of the people.

fugitive One who runs away from the law.

grain elevator A building equipped with mechanical lifting devices for storing grain.

liberal   A person who regards change and reform as progress; usually believes in freedom for the individual.

nativists   People who are prejudiced against persons born in foreign countries.

pacifists   People who oppose war and believe that disputes should be settled peacefully.

plank   A political party's belief about a specific issue.

platform   A party's summary of its principles and specific positions about a particular issue.

primary   An election in which the people choose a political party's candidates.

secede   To formally withdrawal from an organization or group.

sedition   Conduct or language that encourages rebellion against the authority of a government.

tariff   A special tax imposed on imported or exported goods.

BIBLIOGRAPHY

Archer, Jules. *The Incredible Sixties*. San Diego, Calif.: Harcourt Brace, Jovanovich, 1986.

Barr, Roger. *The Vietnam War*. San Diego, Calif.: Lucent Books, 1991.

Blumer, Ronald H. "The Crash of 1929." The American Experience. PBS, 1990.

Bredeson, Carmen. *Ross Perot Billionaire Politician*. Springfield, N.J.: Enslow Publishers, Inc., 1995.

Brookhiser, Richard. *Alexander Hamilton American*. New York: The Free Press, 1999.

Byker, Carl, and David Mrazek. "The Duel." The American Experience. PBS, 2000.

Carter, Dan T. *The Politics of Rage: George Wallace, the Origins of the New Conservatism, and the Transformation of American Politics*. Baton Rouge: Louisiana State University Press, 2000.

Cerami, Charles. *Young Patriots*. Naperville, Ill.: Sourcebooks, 2005.

"Civil Rights." *Time*. September 27, 1963.

Cunningham, Noble E. *The Jeffersonian Republicans: The Formation of Party Organization 1789–1801*. Chapel Hill: University of North Carolina Press, 1957.

Fayer, Steve. "After the Crash of 1929." The American Experience. PBS, 1990.

Foner, Eric. *Free Soil, Free Labor, Free Men.* New York: Oxford University Press, 1970.

Gable, John. *The Bull Moose Years: Theodore Roosevelt and the Progressive Party.* New York: Kennikat Press, 1978.

Grubin, David. "TR: The Story of Theodore Roosevelt." The American Experience. PBS, 1996.

Hastings, Michael, "Ralph Nader; Playing the Spoiler Again," *Newsweek*, June 7, 2004.

Hovde, Ellen and Muffie Meyer. "The Crash of 1929." The American Experience. PBS, 1990.

Isaacs, Jeremy, and Taylor Downing. *Cold War: An Illustrated History, 1945–1991.* Boston: Little, Brown and Company, 1998.

Kruschke, Earl R. *The Encyclopedia of Third Parties in the United States.* Santa Barbara, Calif.: ABC-CLIO, 1991.

Landau, Elaine. *Friendly Foes: A Look at Political Parties.* Minneapolis, Minn.: Lerner Publications Company, 2004.

———. *The 2000 Presidential Election.* New York: Children's Press, 2002.

Lesher, Stephan. *George Wallace: American Populist.* Boston: Addison, Wesley Publishing Company, 1994.

Lennon, Thomas. "Demon Rum." The American Experience. PBS, 1988.

Lutz, Norma Jean. *The History of the Republican Party.* Philadelphia: Chelsea House Publishers, 2000.

McCullough, David. *John Adams.* New York: Simon & Schuster, 2000.

McPherson, Kelly. *Founding Brothers.* MPH Enteretainment, Inc., for the History Channel, 2002.

Mears, Walter. *Deadlines Past*. Kansas City: Andres McMeel Publishing, 2003.

Nachman, Gerald. *Seriously Funny. The Rebel Comedians of the 1950s and 1960s*. New. York: Pantheon Books, 2003.

Ness, Immanuel, and James Ciment. *The Encyclopedia of Third Parties in America*. Armonk, New York: Sharpe Reference, 2000.

Newfield, Jack. "Mississippi Freedom Democratic Party and the 1964 Democratic Convention." ChickenBones: A Journal. http://www.nathanielturner.com/mississippifreedom democraticparty.htm.

Rutland, Robert A. *The Democrats From Jefferson to Carter*. Baton Rouge: Louisiana State University Press, 1979.

Saffell, David C. *The Encyclopedia of U.S. Presidential Elections*. New York: Franklin Watts, 2004.

Schlesinger, Arthur. "Who is Henry A. Wallace?" School of Cooperative Individualism. http://www.cooperativeindividualism .org/schlesinger_wallace_bio.html.

Shane, Scott. "Nader is left With Fewer Votes, and Friends, After '04 Race," *New York Times*, November 6, 2004.

Seelye, Katherine. "Convictions Intact, Nader Soldiers On," *The New York Times*, August 2, 2004.

Smallwood, Frank. *The Other Candidates Third Parties in Presidential Elections*. Hanover, N.H.: University Press of New England, 1983.

"The Spoiler." *Newsweek*, May 8, 1967, p. 39.

Ushan, Michael V. *The 1940s*. San Diego, Calif.: Lucent Books, 1999.

"Wallace's Army: The Coalition of Frustration." *Time*. October 18, 1968, pp. 15–20.

Zinn, Howard. "Eugene V. Debs and the Idea of Socialism." http://www.encyclopedia.com.

Web Sites

"Benjamin Spock," Infoplease
http://www.infoplease.com/ce6/people/A0846317.html

"The Black Panther Party," PBS
http://www.pbs.org/wnet/aaworld/reference/articles/black_
panther_party.html

The Black Panther Party Platform at Hanover College
Department of History
http://history.hanover.edu/courses/excerpts/111bppp.html

"The Black Panthers," Marxists Internet Archive
www.marxists.org/history/usa/workers/black-panthers/

"The *Dred Scott* Decision," The History Place
http://www.historyplace.com/lincoln/dred.htm

"1894 Pullman Strike," Chicago Public Library
www.chipublib.org/004chicago/distasters/pullman_strike.html

"Eugene Victor Debs," Eugene V. Debs Foundation
http://www.eugenevdebs.com

Green Party Election Results, Green Party
http://greens.org/elections/

Kent State Shootings Remembered, CNN.com
http://archives.cnn.com/2000/US/05/04/kent.state.revisit/

The Life of Henry A. Wallace: 1888–1965
http://v1.winrock.org/wallacecenter/wallace/bio.html

Mississippi Freedom Democratic Party (MFDP), Mississippi Humanities Council
http://www.usm.edu/crdp/html/cd/mfdp.htm

Mississippi Freedom Democratic Party: Who is Fannie
Lou Hamer? Congress of Racial Equality
http://users.skynet.be/suffrage-universel/us/uspamfdp.htm

The 1963 Inaugural Address of Governor George C. Wallace, Alabama Department of Archives & History
http://www.archives.state.al.us/govs_list/inauguralspeech.html

The Party of Principle: Libertarian Party
http://www.lp.org/article_85.shtml

Patent Medicines, U-S-History.com
http://www.u-s-history.com/pages/h919.html

Photo Essay on the Great Depression, University of Illinois at Urbana-Champaign
http://www.english.uiuc.edu/maps/depression/photoessay.htm

Program of the Communist Party USA
http://www.cpusa.org/article/static/758/

The Prohibition Party
http://www.infoplease.com/ce6/history/A0840237.html

The Pullman Strike
http://siml/library/PullmanStrike.htm

Third World Traveler
http://www.thirdworldtraveler.com/Heroes/EugeneDebsSocialism.html

FURTHER READING

Bonner, Mike. *How to Become an Elected Official*. Philadelphia, Chelsea House Publishers, 2000.

Cunningham, Kevin. *Power to the People*. Chanhassen, Minn.: The Child's World, 2005.

Goldman, David J. *Presidential Losers*. Minneapolis, Minn.: Lerner Publications Company, 2004.

Landau, Elaine. *Friendly Foes: A Look at Political Parties*. Minneapolis, Minn.: Lerner Publications Company, 2004.

———. *The 2000 Presidential Election*. New York: Children's Press, 2002.

Morin, Isobel V. *Politics, American Style*. Brookfield, Conn.: Twenty First Century Books, 1999.

PICTURE CREDITS

INDEX

ABOUT THE AUTHOR

VICKI COX is a freelance writer who has published 600 features for newspapers and magazines in 16 states. She has written 10 other children's biographies and has assembled an anthology, *Rising Stars and Ozark Constellations,* which profiles people and places in the Ozarks. She has an M.S. in education, taught public school for 25 years, and was an instructor for Drury University in Springfield, Missouri. She is past president of the Missouri Writers' Guild. She lives in Chicago, Illinois.